SILENT
SHORES

SILENT SHORES

Population Trend of Migrant Shorebirds &
Conservation Issues of Habitat

AARIF K M

P K PRASADAN

PARTRIDGE
A Penguin Random House Company

To order additional copies of this book, contact
Partridge India
000 800 10062 62
orders.india@partridgepublishing.com

www.partridgepublishing.com/india

CONTENTS

ACKNOWLEDGEMENTS

Books are always an outcome of team efforts, and this one is no exception. This project would not have been possible without the unstinted support of people of Kadalundi especially during our field study in KVCR. We take this opportunity to express our heartfelt thanks to all who had supported and encouraged us in KVCR. The authors are thankful to the Kerala State Department of Forest and Wildlife for providing permission to carry out research work at Kadalundi-Vallikkunnu Community Reserve.

Dr Aarif is thankful to University Grants Commission, Govt of India for providing financial support in the form of Moulana Azad National Fellowship to carry out this study.

We would like to express our deep sense of gratitude to Dr M Nasser, Associate Professor and Head, Department of Zoology, University of Calicut for his constant and continuous support and for critically going through the manuscript. The authors are also indebted to Dr Sabir Bin Muzaffar, Faculty of UAE University, Al Ain UAE and Dr S. Babu, Scientist, Salim Ali Centre for Ornithology and Natural History for their support in statistical analyses of data.

We do express our respectful regards and very sincere gratitude to Dr Tomohiro Kuwae, Scientist, Port and Airport Research Institute, JAPAN, for sharing his valuable ideas, findings and experiences on behavioural ecology of migrant shorebirds and for encouraging us.

We do thank Dr Eelke O. Folmer, University of Groningen, Netherlands, Taej Mundkur, Dr Ilya Maclean Dr Humphrey Sitter, Dr Marine Korosy and Dr Hab Magdalena for their sincere support. Thanks are also due to Dr Manasori Sato, Dr Suzuki, Dr Goldin Qudrus and Dr M.Moosa for identifying the prey animals and for analyzing the prey samples.

We also acknowledge the services of Dr Harikumar and Dr Madhavan Komath of Centre for Water Resources Development and Management, Calicut in analyzing the water samples.

Sincere affection, care, love, patience and unstinted support extended by the wife of Dr Aarif Ms Fathima Shadiya K, son Hatim Noraiz, his parents-in-law (Mr Alavi K and Mrs Mini PC), grandfather Mr Hussain PC and brother-in-law Mr Shabeersha are gratefully acknowledged. Without their constant support this humble effort would not have born fruit. The care concern and constant criticism in science and life extended by Dr Sudha Devi A R, wife of Dr Prasadan are also thankfully acknowledged.

We are grateful to Dr Adal Arasan IFS, Divisional Forest Officer; Mr Prabakaran, Forest Ranger, KVCR in-charge and Mr Kunjali and local people of Kadalundi especially Mr Hamsakoya, Mr Jafer and Mr. Jamsheed for their whole hearted co-operation and help during the field study.

PREFACE

Declining trend in the population of many species of transcontinental migrant shorebirds is an issue of global conservation concern. As the migrant shorebirds travel very long distance across different frontiers and continents they have to face a plethora of threats and challenges. Moreover, any sort of hindrances/hurdles in any part of their flyways would consequently increase their vulnerability. Through this book we are trying to address these global issues by projecting Kadalundi Vallikkunnnu Community Reserve (KVCR), an important stop over site in the Central Asian Flyway, as a model.

The main objective of bringing out a book of this sort is to popularize the story of transcontinental migrant shorebirds visiting the West Coast region of India. The book focuses mainly on two major issues (on the basis of thorough scientific study):

1. The shorebirds are ecological indicators of wetland health on a global scale. It is a matter of serious international conservation concern that shorebird populations are declining all over the world, with many species and populations facing imminent threats of endangerment or extinction. The population of migrant shorebirds coming to our West Coast has been declining drastically. This finding is an outcome of dedicated and systematic scientific investigation (as a part of the doctoral work of Dr Aarif) made in the West Coast focusing on Kadalundi-Vallikkunnu Community reserve (KVCR). KVCR, one of the four Community Reserves in India, supports transcontinental migratory shorebirds in Central Asian Flyway (CAF). The CAF covers

30 countries of which India is one of the dominant wintering grounds for shorebirds.

2. Shorebirds can be regarded as global sentinels of environmental changes due to their migratory ecology and habitat use patterns. For long-distant migrants, the ecological quality of wintering ground appears to be of key importance. The West Coast of India faces environmental threats due to anthropogenic activities. Habitat destruction, solid waste dumping, sand mining, and so on are subjected to scientific study in KVCR. The role of man-made infrastructures in/near the habitat like roads, bridges, mobile towers etc were also subjected to study. The consequences of these anthropogenic activities on the survival of macrobenthic invertebrates (major prey items of shorebirds) and their habitats have been studied following proven scientific methods. The dominance of humans and their population explosion are likely to competitively exclude many species of migrant shorebirds. Declining food resources and reduced suitability of stop-over sites have far reaching implications on the reproduction and survival of migrant shorebirds. Climate change due to anthropogenic activities may exacerbate the situation. The book focuses on the major environmental threats and suggests specific management plans for reducing the cumulative impacts on West Coast in General and Kadalundi-Vallikkunnu Community Reserve in particular.

If the anthropogenic pressures on this ideal stopover site of transcontinental migrant shorebirds continue to escalate at the same pace, the winged visitors may find other suitable habitats for wintering and foraging. ***The music of the fluttering wings may be silenced if we do not wake up to this dire situation. The authors are apprehensive of this Silence settling on the Shores all over the world.***

CHAPTER ONE

MIGRANT BIRDS, THEIR FLYWAYS AND HABITATS

Migration – still a mystery.......!

Bird migration, the seasonal movement of birds from their breeding grounds to their wintering grounds, is perhaps one of the most spectacular, physically demanding, and mysterious wildlife events and is one of the most compelling aspects of the avian world. Billions of birds migrate vast distances across the globe, twice a year. Typically, these journeys follow a predominantly North-South axis, linking breeding grounds in arctic and temperate regions with non-breeding sites in temperate and tropical areas. Some birds are physically designed for long, rapid flight.

A series of questions crop up in our mind when we start to think about the mystery of bird migration. How and why do birds migrate? How do they find their way across such long distances? Why do they travel in swarms of hundreds to thousands? How do they know when to leave for either their breeding or wintering areas? Scientist still have not understood all aspects of migration. It can be interpreted that migration is a strategy that has evolved over time as conditions in the Earth's geography and climate changed. One theory suggests that as the last Ice Age ended and northern areas began to experience warmer weather, short summers favored insects because of their short life spans and rapid breeding cycles. Some birds moved towards north to take advantage of this abundant food source and because there were fewer species to compete for food. Soon natural selection took hold. The birds that were most efficient at migrating arrived at the breeding grounds first and were more likely to reproduce and raise young successfully.

Flyways– the highways in the sky

The migratory routes of birds, referred to as flyways are general routes that most migrants tend to follow. Through these highways in the sky they fly from their breeding grounds in the north to more southern areas where they spend their winters. Biologists have determined migration routes through the use of radio telemetry and observation of banded and flagged birds. For some species, they can even tell where birds are from by their bill length and coloration.

Most migrating birds require the presence of wetlands in their breeding habitat and on their wintering grounds. These two regions are often thousands of miles apart. Shorebirds depend on wetlands in between for food and rest to reach their final destinations. Large numbers of migrating shorebirds will return to the same stopover site year after year.

Many species migrate along broadly similar, well-established routes known as flyways[1]. The Central Asian Flyway (CAF) is the shortest flyway in the world lying entirely within the Northern Hemisphere[2, 3]. The CAF is utilized by wader populations that breed in the Central Siberian Arctic, boreal Russia and the Central Asian steppe (long and medium-distance migrants), with short-distance migrants and residents breed in the South of Himalayan mountain chain. Under current population delimitations there is a considerable overlap of migratory populations with the West Asian/East African Flyway and some with the East Asian/Australasian Flyway. The wintering ground for long and medium distance migrants are poorly known, but are believed to be chiefly inland freshwater and saline wetlands in Central Asian countries. Wintering areas are mostly coastal intertidal wetlands from Eastern Pakistan to Myanmar, and some birds continue on to Indian Ocean islands. Major coastal wintering areas include the Indus Delta (Pakistan), the NW Indian Coast, the SW Indian/ Sri Lankan Coast, the Bangladesh Coast and probably deltas on the Coast of Myanmar.

The CAF comprises of several important and overlapping migration routes for different species of waterbirds, most of which extend from Siberia to South West Asia[4]. CAF connects a large swathe of the Palearctic with the Indian subcontinent. Separating the subcontinent from the Tibetan Plateau to the North are the Himalayas, which rise to over eight kilometers and stretch 200 kilometers from North to South. Many migratory birds that breed in the mid-Palearctic choose to avoid this formidable barrier and instead make a longer South-Westerly flight to Africa for the Northern winter. There are, however, several Palearctic breeders that do migrate to South Asia. Most of them 'squeeze' into the Indian subcontinent via routes at the two ends of the Tibetan massif. Others, like the Bar-headed Goose, follow a route directly over the Himalayan range. The species is the world's highest-altitude migrant, capable of clearing even Mount Everest[1].

The flyway is also important for migratory waders, with arctic-breeding species travelling from North and Central Siberia to winter in South Asia, principally along the East Coast of India. Some species, such as the Great Knot (VU), even migrate to the subcontinent from far Eastern Siberia. Many wader species, including the Curlew Sandpiper and Little Stint, appear to undertake a loop migration, entering India through the North and North-West during early autumn, before moving South-East to the East Coast of India. In spring they pass back to North along India's East Coast[1]. The CAF covers 30 countries of which India is one of the dominant wintering grounds for shorebirds. The flyway is mostly land locked and it overlaps with East-Asian-Australian-Flyway & African-Eurasian-Flyway.

Wetlands - the most preferred stopover sites

Wetlands play an important role in maintaining the biodiversity as they abode many species of plants and animals mainly due to their large habitat diversity. Birds are the most noticeable wetland animal species that are really sensitive to hydrological changes.[5] These birds are one of the top level predators in the food chain and play a vital role in the sustenance of their ecosystem[6]. Among the wetland birds, shorebirds are the important group of migrants[7]. Shorebirds (migrant birds that forage at sea shore) are different from sea birds (birds that spend most of their life out at sea) and wading birds (taller birds that wade in wetland for their food). They are found in shallow water at coastal as well as inland wetlands and play a significant role in maintaining the

3

health of the environment[8]. Several species of shorebirds are distant migrants[9]. Shorebirds are small to medium sized waders characterized by having slender body, probing bills, pointed wings and long legs. Most shorebirds are migratory and they usually wade close to the shore and poke their bills into the ground in search of food. They are represented by the sandpipers, plovers, jacanids, snipes, curlews, lapwings, godwits, ruffs, dowitchers, avocets, thick-knees, coursers and stilts. They are some of the most amazing migrants of the world, making 'round trip' from the high arctic to South America, Australia, Africa and widely scattered islands of the Pacific, and visits the same sites every year. They used to visit wetlands and marshes (the habitats that are disappearing at a rapid rate) and are considered as biological indicators of ecosystem health. Many species are poorly known. Field identification of migrant shorebirds is tremendously challenging and each species demonstrates an exquisite example of resource partitioning, or ecological nichemanship.

Kadalundi Bird Sanctuary-a haven for winged visitors

Kadalundi bird sanctuary lies in Malappuram district of Kerala State in India. It spreads over a cluster of islands that covers an area of 3Kms surrounded by hillocks. A hillock which is 200 m above sea level provides a splendid view to this marvelous spot. It is the most attractive bird sanctuary in Kerala and is located at a distance of 19 kms from Kozhikode district headquarters and 7 kms from Beypore Port. Kadalundi bird sanctuary is the haven that provides shelter to more than a hundred species of native birds. Over 60 species of migratory birds flock here in large numbers. The place is also famous for a wide variety of edible fish, mussels and crabs which inhabit the neighbouring water bodies. The ideal period to visit this sanctuary in all its glory is from November to April.

Shorebirds can be seen on almost every shoreline and on many other biotopes all over the world. These attractive birds are of economic and ecological importance and, therefore, form a subject of intensive study in some parts of the world[10]. Population status of shorebirds can be taken as an indicator of environment health. We cannot think of conserving shorebirds in isolation without planning to conserve their habitats, the wintering ground or stopover sites. Regrettably, however, the loss and degradation of wetlands and other habitats continue apace all around the world[11], and are the underlying causes of the poor conservation status of so many species. Habitat changes have complex ecological, demographic and genetic consequences for waders[10]. The order Charadriiformes (shorebirds) is a large order and is widely distributed throughout the world. Their ecology and foraging behaviour had been a subject of intensive investigation in many parts of the globe[12, 13, 14, 15].

Shorebirds relish diverse macrobenthic invertebrates that include polychaetes, crustaceans, aquatic insects, insect larvae etc. available in their wintering stopover sites. They forage either individually or in scattered flocks on wet intertidal flats, usually away from the borderline of waterbodies[16]. Birds procure different types/species of prey from the same area without competing with each other as the prey of each bird species inhabits at different depths in the substrata. Moreover, the shape and length of beaks in each species is unique, and therefore, each bird species follow its own mode of foraging[17]. Shorebirds usually detect/locate their prey by visual and tactile sensory mechanisms and exhibit a wide range of feeding styles such as pecking, probing, stabbing, sweeping and ploughing[17]. Their habitat selection depends on the prey availability as well as the foraging strategy[18]. Hyperphagy (excessive eating) is a characteristic feature recognized in many arctic-breeding species of shorebirds[19].

As mentioned earlier, the shorebirds are ecological indicators of wetland health on a global scale[20]. Shorebird populations worldwide are in a perilous state, with 48% of the 200 populations with known trends in decline[21]. These declines are troubling because shorebirds are likely to be important indicators of wetland health on a global scale. Typically, extrinsic threats such as habitat loss, predation, climate change, and hunting are cited as the major probable causes of population decline or elevated extinction risk across many taxa. Many long-distance migrating shorebird (i.e., sandpipers, plovers, flamingos, oystercatchers) populations are declining. With the support of their findings in an extensive study, Wader Study Group[21] pointed out that shorebirds are declining very rapidly at a global scale. In India shorebirds are decreasing in number due to anthropogenic pressure on potential habitats in CAF.

West Coast-more productive but least explored

There are two coasts in the Indian subcontinent: West Coast and East Coast. In the East Coast, Gulf of Mannar[22], Point Calimere[23], Pichavaram[24], Pulicate lake[3] and Chilka lake[25] are the important wintering and stop over grounds for migrant shorebirds[3]. The Population structure of shorebirds is well studied in Point Calimere[23], Pichavaram[24], Chilka[25] and Pulicat lake[3] in the East Coast, whereas, in the West Coast no such published information is available on the shorebird population trends and structure. Even then it is established that West Coast is more productive than East Coast of India[26].

Two hundred and fourteen species of shorebirds belonging to 14 families were recorded all over the world[21], and in India about 49 species of migrant shorebirds[27] were documented. There are 38 species in the recorded list of shorebirds in the West Coast[28, 29, 30, 31, 32, 33] and 45 species in the East Coast[34, 6, 3]. However, in Kadalundi 31 species [35] were reported.

It is a very serious matter of international conservation concern that shorebird populations are declining all over the world, with many species facing imminent threat of endangerment or extinction[21, 36, 37]. On different flyways, an estimated shorebird population between 33% and 68% are in decline (overall 48%), when there is only 0-29% increase (overall 16%). Thus three times as many populations are in decline as are in increase. The reasons for this population decline are diverse but habitat loss or degradation[38] may contribute to this significantly. The expansion and dominance of human population are likely to competitively exclude many species[37] with major changes in the distribution and abundance of living biota. Climate change due to anthropogenic activities is predicted to exacerbate the situation[37]. Shorebirds can be regarded as global sentinels of such environmental changes due to their migratory ecology and habitat use patterns[39]. Declining food resources and reduced suitability of stop-over sites have far reaching implications for the survival and reproduction of migrant shorebirds[21]. For long-distant migrants, the ecological quality of wintering ground appears to be of key importance[10].

Natural wildlife Action plans of Government of India adopted in 2002 emphasises the significance of people's participation and their supports for wildlife conservation. They have made four categories of Protected Areas such as National Parks, Wildlife Sanctuaries, Conservation Reserves and Community Reserves. Accordingly, a network of 668 Protected Areas (PAs) has been established extending over a 1661221.57 KM^2 (4.90% of total geographic area) comprising 102 National Parks, 515 Wildlife Sanctuaries, 47 Conservation Reserves and four Community Reserves. Conservation Reserves (UN Category VI) are community co-managed biodiversity rich areas that are particularly close to the existing Protected Area and serve as buffer and/

or corridor to establish a continuous Protected Area Network[40]. Conservation Reserves can be declared only on Government-owned lands[41]. Community Reserves (IUCN Category V), on the other hand, can be set up on biodiversity abundant lands that are privately or community-owned, and are managed by individual(s)/communities in possession of the area. Both these reserves permit extraction of natural resources, and the levels of which are governed by a multi-stakeholder Reserve Management Committee[42].

Let us quote the description given by the Ministry of Environment and Forests (MoEF) Government of India: "*Community Reserves can be declared by the State Government in any private or community land, not comprised within a National park, Sanctuary or a Conservation Reserve, where an individual or community has volunteered to conserve wildlife and its habitat. Community Reserves are declared for the purpose of protecting fauna, flora, and traditional or cultural conservation values and practices. As in the case of a Conservation Reserve the rights of people living inside a community reserve are not affected*". The Community Reserve comes under Category VI recognized by United Nations. Currently there are four community reserves in India having a size range between 1.5KM^2 (Kadalundi-Vallikkunnu Community Reserve, Kerala) and 12.67km^2 (Lalwan Community Reserve, Punjab).

Kadalundi-Vallikkunnu Community Reserve (KVCR)-a global model

The KVCR (11°7'28"– 11°8'01"N and 75°49'36"–75°50'20"E, (Plate 1 a) is located at the mouth of the River Kadalundi that drains into the Arabian Sea on the West Coast of Kerala. Before entering the sea the river divides into two channels that encircle a small island. The raised sandbars on the western and southern sides of the island separate the lagoon from the sea[43]. Apart from scattered patches of mangroves, the estuary is bordered by coconut groves and human habitation. Around eight hectares of mudflat - exposed during low tides - offer potential foraging ground for several hundreds of wintering and resident waterbirds, particularly shorebirds. The area provides significant socio-economic and livelihood services (fishing, oyster farming and sand mining) to the people living around the estuary.

KVCR is one of the most important wintering and stop-over grounds for migrant shorebirds in the West Coast of India[43, 44]. No in depth studies on the foraging ecology of migrant shorebirds were undertaken in KVCR and no published information is available on their population trends so far. The KVCR supports transcontinental migratory shorebirds similar to other known wetlands such as Kole Wetland in Kerala, Chilka Lake in Orissa, Pulicate Lake in Andhra Pradesh and Point Calimere, Great Vedarnayam swamp, Gulf of Mannar & Pichavaram mangroves in Tamil Nadu[28]. The Intertidal flats in KVCR are important feeding and roosting habitats, especially as stopovers for many migrant shorebirds.

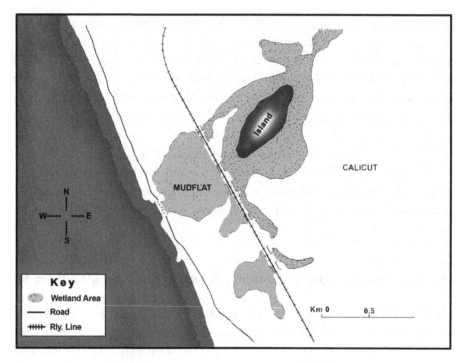

Plate 1 a: Kadalundi-Vallikkunnu Community Reserve (KVCR)

Five major habitat types were identified in KVCR for our study - mudflats, mangroves, shallow water in mangroves, shallow water in mudflats and sand beaches.

Mudflats

Mudflats or tidal flats are common coastal wetlands that are formed when mud is deposited by tide. Generally mudflats are fully exposed during low tide (Plate 2). The vertical stratum of soil in this habitat is arranged in the following sequence: first 5cm contain mud, while the second and third 5 cm strata contains mud with very fine sand and mud with large sand grains respectively.

Plate 2: Mudflat

Mangroves

Mangroves are various large and extensive types of trees that grow up to a medium height and shrubs that grow in saline coastal sediment habitat. In Kadalundi the mangrove forests are located in the eastern side of the mudflat (Plate 3). Seven species - *Avecennia officinalis, A. marina, Rhizophora mucronata, Kandelia candel, Brugeria cylindrica, Acanthus ilicifolius and Excocecaria agalloch* dominate in KVCR[45].

Plate 3: Mangrove

Shallow water in mangroves and mudflats

Mudflats are fully exposed during low tide, at the same time certain areas of mudflats maintain small pools of water (Plate 4 a & b) during pre-monsoon, monsoon and post-monsoon seasons and hence this area may be treated as a different habitat. The same type of habitat is seen near mangroves and that are represented by mangrove creeks and shallow water.

Plate 4 a: Shallow Water in Mudflats

Plate 4 b: Shallow Water in Mangroves

Sand beaches

The sand beaches are located at approximately 1.5 kms away from the KVCR (Plate 5). During the study we have selected 1.2 kms long transect of sand beach for bird sampling. The Northern border of the sand beach is a boat landing site and the Southern border is a Panchayath road. Local fishermen settlements are located adjacent to the sampling area and very close to the Panchayath Road.

Plate 5: Sand beach

KVCR gets water from Kadalundi River

The main source of water to the Community Reserve area is the Kadalundi River. Its tributaries and small rivulets supply water to the entire area. The Kadalundi River is the confluence of its two main tributaries *viz*. the Olipuzha and the Veliyar. The Olipuzha takes its origin from 'the Cherakkombban Mala' (1160 msl) and the Veliyar originates from the forest of the 'Erattakomban Mala' (1190 msl), in the Malappuram district. The Kadalundi River is 130 kms long with a drainage area of 1274 sq. km. The river joins the Lakshadweep Sea at about 5 kms south of the Chaliyar river mouth. It is worth mentioning here that salt water intrusion is one of the major reasons that delimit the availability of drinking water in the Community Reserve area.

Weather

In KVCR, December to May is the dry season and the hottest period is February to May. The temperature ranges between a minimum of 23.04⁰ C in January to a maximum of 38.31⁰C in May. Even though the area receives both South West and North East monsoons the bulk of the annual rainfall is from the South West monsoon. The tract gets a few pre-monsoon showers in April and an average rainfall of about 3166 mm annually. Heavy showers accompanied by thunder and lightning occur in the afternoons during October-November in the North East monsoon. The area experiences strong winds during May, June and July and moderate winds during the rest of the year.

KVCR is endowed with a diverse flora

Besides mangroves, vegetation of the KVCR is represented by 326 species of plants with 168 species of medicinal value, 41 weeds, 29 ornamental plants, 26 crops, 11 timber species and so on[46]. The important mangrove species in KVCR are given in Table 1:

Table 1: Mangrove species of KVCR

S. No	Scientific Name	Common Name
1	*Acanthus ilicifolius* L	Sea Holly Mangrove
2	*Aegiceras corniculata* (L) Balco	River Mangrove
3	*Avicennia marina* (Forssk.) Vierh	Grey Mangrove
4	*Avicennia officinalis* L	White Mangrove
5	*Bruguiera cylindrica* (L) Blume	Small leaved Orange Mangrove
6	*Excoecaria agallocha* L	Blind your eye Mangrove
7	*Rhizophora mucronata* Poir.	Long fruited stilted Mangrove
8	*Sonneratia alba*	Nakshatra kandal, Mangrove apple
9	*Kandelia candel*	Nallakandal

Faunal diversity of KVCR is rich

The fauna in KVCR is dominated by 15 species of mammals, 109 species of birds, 23 species of reptiles, seven species of amphibians, 12 species of fishes and 38 species of butterflies dominate among the noticeable group of animals.

Shorebirds choose K V C R as an ideal stopover site

Migrant shorebirds visit KVCR regularly as this habitat is an ideal stopover site and wintering ground in their flyway. Of the 31 species of shorebirds studied, 25 were Winter Visitors (WV), four Vagrants (V) and two were Local Migrants (LM). Among the 31 migrants, six were 'common species', eight 'fairly common', seven 'uncommon', four 'rare' and six were 'irregular' species. In the 'common' group, the Lesser Sand Plover was the most dominant species (Table 2).

All the 31 species of shorebirds recorded (Table 2) except Little Ringed Plover and Black-winged Stilt are Winter Visitors to this area. Five thousand and forty four (peak at one time) Lesser Sand Plovers were recorded at KVCR followed by Kentish Plover and Common Redshank. Black winged Stilt, Broad- billed Sandpiper and Green Sandpiper were lesser in number than other migrant shorebirds. Three species of shorebirds - Spotted Redshank, Pied Avocet and Crab Plover - were excluded from the study as their presence was irregular and unpredictable.

Out of the 31 species of migrant shorebirds studied, 25 come under the 'Least Concern category' of IUCN, four 'Near Threatened', one 'Vulnerable' and one endangered.

Table 2-Distribution of Shorebirds in the KVCR, their Threat Category, Migratory Status, Global Population Threshold and Estimated Global Population:

Common Name	Scientific Name	IUCN Status	KVCR Status	Migration Status	Peak Count (one time)	1% Global population (Global Threshold)	Estimated Global Population
Haematopodidae							
Eurasian Oystercatcher	*Haematopus ostralegus*	VU	Rare	V	2	1500	100,000-200,000
Charadriidae							
Lesser Sand Plover	*Charadrius mongolus*	LC	Common	WV	5044	1250	100,000-150,000
Greater Sand Plover	*Charadrius leschenaultii*	LC	Fairly Common	WV	339	1000	100,000
Little Ringed Plover	*Charadrius dubius*	LC	Uncommon	R/LM	21	1000	100,000
Kentish Plover	*Charadrius alexandrinus*	LC	Common	WV	637	750	50,000-100,000
Pacific Golden Plover	*Pluvialis fulva*	LC	Fairly Common	WV	350	750	50,000-100,000
Grey Plover	*Pluvialis squatarola*	LC	Uncommon	WV	19	750	30000
Scolopacidae							
Common Snipe	*Gallinago gallinago*	LC	Irregular	WV	8	1000	100,000
Black-tailed Godwit	*Limosa limosa*	NT	Fairly Common	WV	22	1500	150,000
Bar-tailed Godwit	*Limosa lapponica*	NT	Uncommon	WV	39	1300	130000
Whimbrel	*Numenius phaeopus*	LC	Common	WV	81	1000	100,000
Eurasian Curlew	*Numenius arquata*	NT	Fairly Common	WV	24	1000	100,000
Spotted Redshank	*Tringa erythropus*	LC	Irregular	V	1	250	25000
Common Redshank	*Tringa totanus*	LC	Common	WV	368	1000	100,000
Marsh Sandpiper	*Tringa stagnatilis*	LC	Irregular	WV	3	1000	100,000
Common Greenshank	*Tringa nebularia*	LC	Common	WV	82	2,300	190,000-270,000

Green Sandpiper	*Tringa ochropus*	LC	Rare	WV	8	1000	100,000
Wood Sandpiper	*Tringa glareola*	LC	Rare	WV	12	1500	100,000-200,000
Terek Sandpiper	*Xenus cinereus*	LC	Fairly Common	WV	76	1000	100,000
Common Sandpiper	*Actitis hypoleucos*	LC	Common	WV	19	750	75000
Ruddy Turnstone	*Arenaria interpres*	LC	Fairly Common	WV	23	1000	100,000
Great Knot	*Calidris tenuirostris*	EN	Uncommon	WV	9	35	2,000-5,000
Sanderling	*Calidris alba*	LC	Fairly Common	WV	51	1000	100,000
Little Stint	*Calidris minuta*	LC	Fairly Common	WV	23	2500	200,000-300,000
Temminck's Stint	*Calidris temminckii*	LC	Rare	WV	16	1000	100,000
Dunlin	*Calidris alpina*	LC	Uncommon	WV	23	1000	100,000
Curlew Sandpiper	*Calidris ferruginea*	NT	Uncommon	WV	41	2500	200,000-300,000
Broad-billed Sandpiper	*Limicola falcinellus*	LC	Uncommon		WV	8	1000	100,000
Recurvirostridae							
Black-winged Stilt	*Himantopus himantopus*	LC	Irregular	LM	7	1750	150,000-200,000
Pied Avocet	*Recurvirostra avosetta*	LC	Irregular	V	1	1000	100,000
Dromadidae							
Crab Plover	*Dromas ardeola*	LC	Irregular	V	1	1750	60,000-80,000

The main wintering grounds for the shorebirds that make use of the Central Asian/South Asian Flyway are located in India, especially along the East Coast[2]. Although the population of shorebirds has been found declining in the East Coast, the actual reasons for that are poorly understood[3]. The Central Asian flyway is the poorly known flyway for a high proportion of its shorebird population and nothing is known about its population size or its trend[3]. Findings of the IWSG[21], revealed that majority of shorebirds of the known population trend are in decline all around the world.

India stands forth as one of the important countries for migrant shorebirds in Central Asian Flyway[2]. Seventy species of shorebirds are recorded from India[35], and in Kerala 31 species were recorded from Kadalundi. It clearly emphasizes the conservation significance of West Coast in general and KVCR in particular. There are probably many contributing factors for the widespread decline in shorebirds. The most likely driver of recent decline appears to be habitat loss in staging areas[47, 48]. The declining species reported were diverse in their resource requirements, varying greatly in both food preferences during the non-breeding season and in the selection of breeding habitats in Northern Hemisphere[47, 48]. The most obvious and widespread shared threat that this diverse group of shorebirds face is the rapid destruction of intertidal habitats[49, 50].

Arrival begins in August and return commences in January

The migrants were found to arrive during the middle of August to the first week of March. The number of shorebirds, except some rare species (unpredictable) was highest during the months of December and January (Table 3). Lesser Sand Plover (Plate 6) is the first species that arrives at KVCR in a year followed by Kentish Plover, Common Redshank and Terek Sandpiper. The return journey of shorebirds begins during the last week of January to the last of week of May (Table 3).

Plate 6: Lesser Sand Plover

A comparison between the West Coast and East Coast on the basis of the arrival departure pattern of shorebirds at KVCR revealed some interesting results. Of the 31 species of shorebirds recorded in the present study, only 21 species were found in the East Coast. The arrival time of migrant shorebirds is usually the middle of August to the first week of March in the West Coast, whereas, in the East Coast, it starts in the first week of August and goes up to the second week of May. The departure time is the last week of January to the last week of May in the West Coast. On the other hand, it is the second week of April to the first week of May in the East Coast (Table 3).

Pied Avocet is a regular visitor in the East Coast, whereas it is a rare winter visitor in the West Coast. Another rare winter visitor of West Coast, the Spotted Redshank has been reported as regular in the East Coast. The story of the Greater Sand Plover is a different one. It visits the West Coast regularly, at the same time the bird has not been recorded in the East Coast.

Table 3-Arrival and Departure of Migrant Shorebirds in KVCR during 2005 to 2012:

S. No	Species	Month of Arrival	Month of Departure
1	Eurasian Oystercatcher	Unpredictable	Unpredictable
2	Lesser Sand Plover	Middle of August to first week of September	Middle of May to last week of May
3	Greater Sand Plover	Last week of September to middle of October	Last week of April to last of week May
4	Little Ringed Plover	First week of January to middle of February	Last week of March to middle of April
5	Kentish Plover	Last week of September to first week of October	Last week of April to last week of May
6	Pacific Golden Plover	Last week of November to first week of January	Last week of April to first week of May
7	Grey Plover	Middle of September to first week of October	Last week of March to first week of April
8	Common Snipe	Unpredictable	Unpredictable
9	Black- tailed Godwit	Middle of October to first week of December	First week of March to last week of March
10	Bar-tailed Godwit	Middle of November to first week of December	First week of March to first week of April
11	Whimbrel	Middle of September to first week of November	Middle of April to last week of April
12	Eurasian Curlew	First week of October-middle of November	Last week of March to middle of April
13	Spotted Redshank	Unpredictable	Unpredictable
14	Common Redshank	First week of September to last of October	Middle week of April to middle of May
15	Marsh Sandpiper	Unpredictable	Unpredictable
16	Common Greenshank	First week of September to middle of October	Middle of April to first of May
17	Green Sandpiper	Unpredictable	Unpredictable
18	Wood Sandpiper	Unpredictable	Unpredictable
19	Terek Sandpiper	First week of September to first of November	Middle of March to last week of April
20	Common Sandpiper	First week of August to First week of September	First week of May to last week of May

21	Ruddy Turnstone	First week of October to middle of November	Last week of March to first week of April
22	Great Knot	First week of November to first week of December	Middle of January to first week of February
23	Sanderling	Middle of October to first week of November	Middle of April to middle of May
24	Little Stint	First week of September to middle of November	First week of February to last week of March
25	Temminck's Stint	Unpredictable	Unpredictable
26	Dunlin	First week of December to first week of March	Middle of the March to middle of April
27	Curlew Sandpiper	First of week October to first of November	First of week February to last of March
28	Broad-billed Sandpiper	First week of January to middle of February	Middle of February to last week of February
29	Black-winged Stilt	First week of February to first of March	First week of March to last week of March
30	Pied Avocet	Unpredictable	Unpredictable
31	Crab Plover	Unpredictable	Unpredictable

Analyses of the data on the arrival and departure time of shorebirds in the West Coast and East Coast of India indicated a clear cut variation in the commencement of arrival as well as departure. For example the arrival time of Eurasian Curlew in the West Coast is the first week of October to the middle of November. On the other hand, that of East Coast is second week of December. Similarly the commencement of departure of same bird in the West Coast is last week of March to the middle of April. Most of the other migrant shorebird species that forage in the East and West Coasts of India also exhibit similar patterns of arrival- departure clock. A bird-wise comparison of the arrival and departure in both the coasts is not possible as the records in the East Coast is partially incomplete (Table 4). This variation may be linked to the arrival of South West Monsoon and its impacts on the local weather. Normally, in the West Coast, South West monsoon begins in the first week of June and fades away by the end of September, whereas, in the East Coast the monsoon begins in October and fades away by the end of December[3]. The relative abundance of shorebirds during the post monsoon season in both the coasts might be related to the availability of food, and the availability of other habitat requirements for the bird species. The present study and studies carried out in other parts of India[3] clearly indicated that the most ideal arrival period for the migrant shorebirds in the post monsoon season is after September in the West Coast and after December in the East Coast of India.

Over-summering species of shorebirds

The phenomenon in which birds remain on their non-breeding or wintering grounds during their breeding season is over-summering. This phenomenon has been exhibited by many species of shorebirds that come under the families Charadriidae and Scolopacidae[51].

A total of 3233 over-summering shorebirds belonging to seven species (Lesser Sand Plover, Greater Sand Plover, Kentish Plover, Whimbrel, Common Sandpiper, Pacific Golden Plover, Ruddy Turnstone) were recorded from 2005 to 2014 at KVCR. The number of over-summering shorebirds has been found decreasing over the years. Decreasing trend in the number of over-summering shorebirds may be due to the degradation of habitat in the KVCR which must have forced the shorebirds, that are to over-summer, to move to the neighboring wetlands or other suitable habitats in the West Coast itself. Detailed study is needed to establish this hypothesis.

Earlier studies in KVCR[52] documented over-summering in the shorebirds, Greater Sand Plover and Lesser Sand Plover. We could also observe the phenomenon in nine species of shorebirds including Greater Sand Plover and Lesser Sand Plover. Shorebirds observed in June and July were mostly in the non-breeding plumage and could possibly be the sexually immature first-year birds[51].

Table 4-Comparison of arrival and departure data – West and East Coasts of India

S. No	Species	West Coast (Present study)		East Coast (Kannan & Pandiyan 2012)	
		Arrival	Departure	Arrival	Departure
1	Eurasian Oystercatcher	Unpredictable	Unpredictable	Ni	Nil
2	Lesser Sand Plover	Middle of August to first week of September	Middle of May to last week of May	1st week of August	Discontinuously recorded during the study period
3	Greater Sand Plover	Last week of September to middle of October	Last week of April to last week of May	No records	No records
4	Little Ringed Plover	First week of January to middle of February	Last week of March to middle of March	More records in August	Continuously recorded
5	Kentish Plover	Last week of September to first week of October	Last week of April to last week of May	More records in August	Continuously recorded
6	Pacific Golden Plover	Last week of November to first week of January	Last week of April to first week of May	Second week of December	Second week of June
7	Grey Plover	Middle September to first week of October	Last week of March to first week of April	Third week of September	Discontinuously recorded during the study period
8	Common Snipe	First week of September to last week of December	First week of January to last week of January	First week of October	Second week of April
9	Black-tailed Godwit	Middle of October to first week of December	First week of March to last week of March	First week of August	Erratic movements
10	Bar-tailed Godwit	Middle of November to first week of December	First week of March to first week of April	No records	No records
11	Whimbrel	Middle of September to first week of November	Middle of April to last week of April	First week of August	Discontinuously recorded
12	Eurasian Curlew	First week of October-middle of November	Last week of March to middle of April	Second week of December	Continuously recorded
13	Spotted Redshank	Unpredictable	Unpredictable	First week of April	First week of May
14	Common Redshank	First week of September to last of October	Middle week of April to middle of May	Second week of August	First week of May
15	Marsh Sandpiper	Unpredictable	Unpredictable	First week of October	First week of May

16	Common Greenshank	First week of September to middle of October	Middle of April to first of May	First week of August	First week of May
17	Green Sandpiper	Middle of November to middle of December	First week of January to last week of January	No records	No records
18	Wood Sandpiper	Middle of November to last week of December	First week of January to Middle of January	First week of August	First week of April
19	Terek Sandpiper	First week of September to first of November	Middle of March to last week of April	No records	No records
20	Common Sandpiper	First week of August to First week of September	First week of May to last week of May	First week of August	Second week of June
21	Ruddy Turnstone	First week of October to middle of November	Last week of March to first week of April	Second week of May	Single record
22	Great Knot	First week of November to first week of December	Middle of January to first week of February	No records	No records
23	Sanderling	Middle of October to first week of November	Middle of April to middle of May	No records	No records
24	Little Stint	First week of September to middle of November	First week of February to last week of March	First week of August	First week of May
25	Temminck's Stint	First week of January to last week of February	Last week of February to last week of February	First week of October	Second week of April
26	Dunlin	First week of December to first week of March	Middle of the March to middle of April	No records	No records
27	Curlew Sandpiper	First of week October to first of November	First of week February to last of March	First week of December	After which no record of this species
28	Broad-billed Sandpiper	First week of January to middle of February	Middle of February to last week of February	No records	No records
29	Black-winged Stilt	First week of February to first of March	First week of March to last week of March	First week of August	Erratic movements
30	Pied Avocet	Unpredictable	Unpredictable	First week of January	Last week of May and some leaves by First week of May
31	Crab Plover	Unpredictable	Unpredictable	No records	No records

Generally in the arctic and the north temperate regions the juveniles of the shorebirds that winter in the southern hemisphere remain in their winter quarters during their first breeding season. These young shorebirds move towards north only in their second breeding season when they are about 19 months old. It is generally assumed that this situation has arisen because the risks of migration and the low chance of a young bird breeding successfully outweigh the possible benefit of managing to produce young ones. In some species it seems likely that immature ones do not go north to breed until a year later. It is also possible that birds that over-summer in their wintering areas include a few adults that are in poor health. Among the over-summering group of shorebirds, the Lesser Sand Plovers is the most dominant species[53]. Studies on the plumage and the development of gonads of over-summering waders pointed out that gonads are inactive in all over-summering waders and most of them are in non-breeding plumage[54, 55]. Non-breeding plumage is very common among migrant shorebirds[56, 57, 58]. In KVCR all over - summering birds among Lesser Sand Plover, Greater Sand Plover, Kentish Plover, Whimbrel, Common Sandpiper, Pacific Golden Plover, Ruddy Turnstone, Common Redshank and Grey Plover were in non-breeding plumage and appeared to have low mass. Over-summering is related to helminth infestations, to which younger shorebirds are more vulnerable[51]. This would ultimately debilitate the birds and prevent them from migrating back to their breeding ground. We have not made an attempt to study the status of parasitic infestation in migrant shorebirds because collecting and sacrificing of migrant shorebirds are not legally permitted in India. Helminth infestations might be one of the reasons for over-summering in KVCR too. Another possible reason for the presence of very large number of over-summering birds is that it is not worth incurring the risks of a long migration if the possibility of getting success in breeding is low[58]. Although the cost of migrating to different distances has not been quantified, it is generally assumed that the cost of migrating will be greatest for those waders migrating furthest[59, 60]. Thus, for young waders, the timing of return to the breeding grounds for the first time needs to be synchronized with their chances of breeding. All these factors influence the physiological adaptability of the birds for the arduous journey. The arrival of migrant shorebirds at Kadalundi coincides with the reduction of South-West monsoon in September.

Over-summering is a common phenomenon exhibited by many species of shorebirds[53, 61]. Migrant shorebirds in the East Coast are no exception. Earlier studies[61] also documented over-summering in Chilka Lake. Pacific Golden Plover and Terek Sandpiper were found over-summering throughout the year except during June and July. Whimbrels were sighted there throughout the year. Early migrants included Great Knots in flocks of about 500 or more during August to December and Ruff in large numbers as early as October[61]. These timings clearly indicated that these birds are on their way to south India, especially the West Coast.

CHAPTER TWO

HABITAT PREFERENCE

Mudflats – the most preferred habitat

Mudflats in the estuaries are vital feeding grounds for resident bird populations and they provide important overwintering sites for the migratory shorebirds[62]. A high percentage of shorebirds prefer to forage on mudflats, to prey mainly on crustaceans and polychaetes[63, 64]. In Kadalundi also, the exposed mudflats are the primary foraging ground[65, 66]. Shorebirds, whose activities are closely linked to the nature of tides, are affected by time of the day[64] and the number of shorebirds and the duration of their foraging[67, 68] vary with time of day.

Thirty one species of shorebirds were recorded from KVCR during the period from 2005 to 2012. Among the total shorebirds observed in the mudflats of KVCR, the most dominant species was Lesser Sand Plover (81.77 %) followed by Greater Sand Plover (7.5%), Kentish Plover (6.6%) and Pacific Golden Plover (1.2%). The population of shorebirds was found to decline over the years.

Although many species of waterbirds have been recorded from many parts of the globe, the role of intertidal flats as the most preferred habitat for waterbirds has not been well-documented[69]. The Intertidal flats in KVCR are important feeding and roosting habitats, especially as stopovers for migrants that use

Central Asian Flyway and rely on the South China coastal zone as a rest and re-fueling stop. Number of shorebirds visiting KVCR is at its peak during post monsoon months. No shorebirds, except over-summering ones, were recorded during monsoon months[65].

Presence of large flocks of plovers particularly of Lesser Sand Plover and Kentish Plover was a common and marvelous scene during the post monsoon months in KVCR. They were found to arrive in the middle of August to the first week of September; their numbers peaked during December & January and left the estuary by April. Only limited information is available on the seasonal variation in the numbers of migratory shorebirds in South Asia[69]. Earlier studies in KVCR[52] recorded 31 species of migrant shorebirds, of which 29 are of the same species recorded during the present study. Two species, spotted Redshank and Pied Avocet were added to the list in our study. Lesser Sand Plover is an abundant winter visitor, perhaps the most common shorebird to the seaboard from Makran and Sindh in Pakistan, around the entire Peninsula and Bangladesh[70].

The distribution and abundance of prey species is an important factor that determines the distribution of foraging waders on the exposed tidal flats. Selection of foraging areas by shorebirds is related to the distribution and abundance of their prey species[71, 72]. This, in turn, can be linked to the environmental factors such as sediment type[73, 74] and salinity[75], both of which change along an estuarine gradient (i.e. from the head to the mouth). While these are key drivers of broad-scale distribution, waterbirds can also respond to potential foraging habitats at different spatial scales[76], and a suite of additional environmental factors can influence distribution at finer scales. It includes degree of tidal exposure, sediment wetness and relative penetrability[77], the presence of algal mats or the presence and proximity of drainage channels[78, 76].

In KVCR the highest species diversity of shorebirds was recorded on mudflats as in Pulicate Lake[3] and Pichavaram[79] in the East Coast of India. Earlier studies on mudflats revealed that the area selected for most of the studies abodes globally important shorebirds[80, 81, 82, 83, 84]. The birds in large numbers were attracted by a combination of factors that include relatively mild winter and large area of mudflats being exposed due to relatively lower tidal amplitude. Migratory waterbirds like Whimbrel, Eurasian Curlew, Redshank, Asian Dowitcher and Lesser Flamingo as well as several Plover and Sandpiper species were documented from the mudflats at Pichavaram[79].

Habitat preference studies[69] across the world have also indicated the preference of shorebirds for intertidal mudflats provided a strong support to this fact. The highest bird abundance in Leizhou Peninsula was recorded from the intertidal flats and that too accounted for about 69% of the total birds counted. In the coastal wetlands of Leizhou Peninsula of Southern China, species richness and abundance of shorebirds were highest on intertidal flats. Our study revealed that 24 species of migrant shorebirds choose the mudflats of KVCR for foraging.

Stable food supply – essential to maintain regular visit

A stable food supply for shorebirds on tidal flats seems to be important to maintain their regular migration[86]. In a survey made on major Japanese tidal flats during the period from 1988 to 1996, the second highest number of migrating or over-wintering waders (6,950 individuals) was recorded in the estuary that includes Fujimae-higata. Presence of diverse Nereid species with different life cycles patterns on the same tidal flats was reported[86] to enhance their stability as a major food source for migratory shorebirds. The significance of mudflats as excellent foraging grounds for the migrant shorebirds has been emphasized by other workers in the field[2]. During the dry season (December to May), a large area of land was found to get exposed (Nalabana Island) and the exposed land has extensive mudflats that attract over 300 000 waterbirds[2] at Chilka lake.

Mangroves – second in the priority list of winter visitors

The mangrove forests are important wetlands that provide environmental sustainability and ecological security. More than 90% of all marine organisms spend some portion of their life cycle within the mangrove ecosystem[79]. Mangrove swamps, the subtropical and tropical equivalents of the temperate salt marsh, cover at least 14 million hectares worldwide[87]. They are salt tolerant evergreen forests found in the intertidal zones of shores, estuaries, tidal creeks, backwaters, lagoons, marshes and mudflats[88]. The mangroves are important coastal nursery grounds for crustaceans and fishes and their decaying leaves form an important source of nutrients to diverse species of bacteria, zooplankton and phytoplankton. Several species of polychaetes, mollusks and many other invertebrates find shelter in the mangrove ecosystem[79].

Avicennia officinalis, A. marina, Rhizophora mucronata, Kandelia candel, Brugeria cylindrica, Acanthus ilicifolius and *Exocecaria agallocha* are the major mangrove species found in the mangrove wetland of Kadalundi[45]. In KVCR mangroves are the second most important feeding ground for shorebirds. Good number of shorebirds was found foraging on mangrove creeks during low tide[65].

Of the total shorebirds recorded from mangroves 64.2% were Lesser Sand Plovers followed by Pacific Golden Plover (14.7%), Kentish Plover (7.1%), Greater Sand Plover (6.7%), Common Redshank (2.5%) and so on during our study in KVCR. The highest number of Pacific Golden Plovers was recorded from the mangroves. Its number was lesser in the mudflats, shallow water and sand beach. During the study 326 individual Temmincks's Stint (belonging to 'specialist' group), 55 Dunlin and three Little Ringed Plover were also recorded.

Mangrove swamps that enhance the productivity of mudflats and shallow water extends their service as nursery to crabs and fishes and are thus essential, though indirectly, for birds that depend on these food sources[87]. It could be a reason for the shorebirds to congregate at mangroves during the post-monsoon season. Mangrove swamps are essential for the sustenance of productivity of mudflats and shallow coastal water and thereby providing support to birds to make use of these habitats[87]. In the present study, it was found that bird abundance was rich in the mangroves of KVCR. Mangroves serve as an important component of the coastal ecology and because of this factor, the widespread loss and degradation of mangrove forests throughout Southeast Asia and the eastern coast of Australia were subjected for detailed study[89].

Mangroves provide a good habitat for a large number of bird species for feeding and nesting[90, 6, 91]. Indian mangroves alone support 17 species of waterbirds belonging to different threatened categories of IUCN[92]. Mangrove ecosystem commands the highest importance because of its biological productivity and specialized diversity[93]. Among coastal wetlands mangrove forests have higher productivity after coral reef [94]. On the mangroves, the biomass reduction is mainly due to their higher salinity[79]. Higher salinity would have a profound impact on the fauna that includes fungi, plankton, benthic invertebrates, crustaceans, fishes, waterbirds etc.[79]. In fact, copepods are the most important food items of shorebirds[95, 96, 97]. Salinity fluctuations may cause reduction in the diversity of the copepods[79] which in turn causes decline in the number of shorebirds in the study area[98, 99, 100]. Studies[101] have shown that higher salinity in mangroves leads to depletion of nutrients. The reduced availability of nutrients in this habitat might influence the population of plankton, benthic organisms and other macro invertebrates[102]. It is a fact that changes in invertebrate population of any wetland could affect the top level predators such as birds[103].

Shallow water

Many species of shorebirds including Common Redshank, Common Greenshank, Lesser Sand Plover, Bar-tailed Godwit and Curlew Sandpiper prefer shallow water for their foraging activities. The shallow coastal water that provides excellent habitat for the developing young ones of crabs, fishes, etc. are thus essential, though indirectly, for birds that depend on these food sources[87]. At the same time the gregarious Little Stint and Curlew Sandpiper are particularly vulnerable to clap-traps, as they forage on mudflats with shallow water[2]. The significance of shallow water as an ideal habitat for foraging has been studied by many researchers [104, 105, 106, 107]. The seasonal inundation make shallow water and mudflats suitable for foraging by shorebirds[105, 106, 104, 107]. Studies[104] made in other parts of the globe showed that shorebirds generally forage on invertebrates in shallow water.

The highest number of shorebirds recorded from shallow water was Common Redshank followed by Lesser Sand Plover, Common Greenshank, Bar-tailed Godwit, Curlew Sandpiper, Kentish Plover and Black tailed Godwit (Table 7). The highest number (1951) of Common Redshanks was recorded during 2007. Black tailed Godwit (Near Threatened species) generally prefers shallow water for foraging. The highest number (41) recorded was in 2005. This bird was also recorded from the mangroves. Of the 31 species studied the presence of Little Ringed Plover, Pacific Golden Plover, Grey Plover, Common Snipe, Marsh Sandpiper, Green Sandpiper, Wood Sandpiper, Little Stint, Broad Billed Sandpiper, Pied Avocet and Crab Plover was not recorded in shallow water.

The Great Knot (Table 2) which is an uncommon winter visitor at KVCR prefers shallow water and mudflats for foraging. This bird has been categorized as Vulnerable by Bird life International[108] due to its rapid population decline[109]. In South East India, wintering Great Knots in the Gulf of Mannar, have been studied in detail[110]. The species has also been recorded in Goa[111]. In NW India it is described as a 'not abundant but not rare winter visitor' to the Kutch and Kathiawar coast of Gujarat[70].

Water depth – another criterion for habitat selection

Water depth is an important criterion for the migrant shorebirds in selecting their habitat[99]. Most small and medium sized shorebirds forage in shallow water having a depth of <6 cm, while other shorebirds forage in exposed mudflat habitats or in water having a depth of 6 to 15 cms[112]. Shallow water was recognized as the most important indicator/predictor of shorebird abundance within the rainwater basin in Nebraska[113]. There is a strong correlation between the depth of water being selected by waterbirds for foraging and their tarsus length[17]. The long legged Whimbrel and Common Redshank prefer shallow water region, while Lesser Sand Plover with a shorter tarsus prefer to forage in shallow water with less than 6 cm depth.

Along the coast of Ghana[17], waterbirds are most abundant during the dry season when water level in the lagoons falls and the shallow water and exposed mudflats offer favourable conditions for foraging. The Lesser Sand Plover, Common Redshank and Whimbrel prefer a range of water depths up to six cm, nine cm and 14 cm respectively. Available feeding habitats varied from dry mudflats to wet mud and shallow water of no more than 20 cm depth[17]. The highest waterbird diversity is usually found at lower water depth and it can be correlated to hydrological diversity[114, 115, 116, 117, 118, 119].

Size of the bill also plays a significant role in choosing the ideal water depth for foraging. With their short and straight bill small shorebirds like Red-necked Stint is capable of probing to a depth of about two cm while the larger shorebirds like Whimbrel prefers deep probing (deep feeding) and are capable of very deep (> 15 cm) and complex probing of sediment.

Sand banks

About three-quarters of the world's shorelines are sand beaches. Exposed sand beaches accommodate an abundant invertebrate macrofauna[120, 121, 122] which forms an important food source for vertebrate predators such as shorebirds. The sand beaches of Kadalundi, is a rich source of crabs, cosmonotous crabs and occasionally mantis shrimps for shorebirds. Many species of shorebirds prefer sand beaches for feeding activities[123]. Their foraging efficiency in the sand beaches is influenced by many factors including the presence of other animals including man[124]. In Kadalundi, sand beach is a less disturbed area when compared to mudflats, mangroves and shallow water.

In KVCR, Whimbrel and Eurasian Curlew are common in the sand beaches. The highest number (268) of Whimbrel was recorded in 2012. The number of documented Eurasian Curlew was at its highest (400) in the sand beach followed by mudflats (62) and mangroves (39) and lowest (11) from the shallow water body. In the sand beach the highest count (163) recorded was during 2012. Among the Plovers, the Lesser Sand Plover and Kentish Plover are the common species on the sand beach. Of the 31 species observed, the presence of Little Ringed Plover, Common Snipe, Spotted Redshank, Marsh Sandpiper, Green Sandpiper, Wood Sandpiper, Temmincks's Stint, and Pied Avocet was not recorded from the sand beaches. Studies elsewhere[125] showed that Bar-tailed Godwits are generally associated with sandier sediments in contrast to Black-tailed Godwits which favour muddy (silty) sediments, but in Kadalundi maximum number of Black tailed Godwits was observed at shallow water region.

Human activities on the coasts can modify or disturb both waterbirds and their habitats, ultimately influencing waterbird distribution[132]. Given so many variables, the spatial distribution of foraging waders is, therefore, both complex and challenging to understand. Increasing coastal human populations throughout the world will continue to generate conflicts between coastal recreation and shorebird populations because both depend on a very narrow strip of habitat[133]. Conserving the preferred foraging grounds of the shorebirds should be granted maximum priority to arrest the decline in shorebird populations across the shores of the different continents.

CHAPTER THREE

POPULATION TRENDS OF SHOREBIRDS
AND THEIR HABITAT USE

A declining trend in the percentage of birds is evident

A declining trend in many species of shorebirds, including Lesser Sand Plovers, Greater Sand Plovers, Pacific Golden Plovers, Common Sandpipers, Curlew Sandpipers, Wood Sandpipers, Sanderlings and Little Stints visiting mudflats, mangroves and shallow water habitats at KVCR has been observed. At the same time a significant increase in the number of shorebirds has been Recorded on the sand beach (Fig 1 & 2).

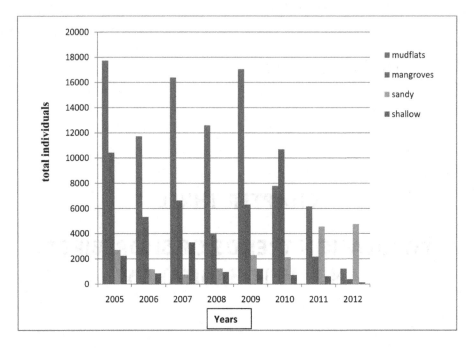

Fig 1: Total number of shorebirds that made use of different habitats in KVCR

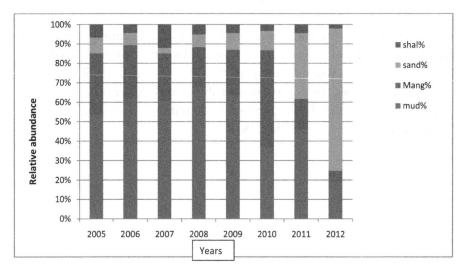

Fig: 2 Relative abundance of shorebirds in different habitat types

Shorebird number decreases with increase in rainfall and the major reason for this may be the changes in the availability of food. Total counts may sometimes be obscure because of variations in the timing of different species of shorebirds flying through, to avoid competition for food and/or of other factors[104].

Habitat preference depends on prey abundance

Habitat use patterns of migrant shorebirds change over time in KVCR. The total shorebird counts indicated a gradual but significant shift in habitat usage from mudflats and mangroves to sand beaches (Fig 1). Lesser Sand Plover continues to be the most abundant species and this may be due to its shift in habitat usage to the less preferred habitat, the sandbeach[65]. The habitat use patterns are reflective of the ecological and behavioral differences among species[64, 134, 135, 136, 65]. Most shorebirds are influenced by the tidal cycle in their feeding habits[134, 137]. Lesser Sand Plovers prey on different species of invertebrates in mudflats, mangroves and sand beaches of the same locality,[65] eventhough polychaete worms are their most preferred prey animals. Polychaete worms are abundant in mudflats, followed by mangroves and are absent in sand beaches. This variation in abundance is significantly related to the mean number of pecks of Lesser Sand Plover in the substrata recorded in the habitats[138, 65]. On the other hand, crabs are present in all the three habitats (mudflats, mangroves and sand beaches), but the corresponding number of pecks declined gradually from mudflats, mangroves to sand beaches. It has been documented that shorebirds are spatially distributed in relation to the prey base[64, 134, 135, 136,] and are found abundantly in areas where their preferred prey is present. for example, White-rumped Sandpipers, whose favourite prey are polychaetes are abundant in areas with the highest densities of polychaetes (Fig 3). The study suggests that high levels of nutrient input and disturbances have an influence on the distribution of benthic communities of the intertidal areas in Kadalundi estuary[139]. Specifically, there has been a reduction in the number and diversity of polychaetes (Fig 3) which could be associated with nutrient enrichment[136, 139]. For many shorebird species, reduction in polychaetes is in tune with poor quality of habitat. Such a situation has forced the shorebirds to shift to sand beaches, in recent years. Similar findings have been reported from many parts of the globe[137, 135, 136].

Other migrant birds (Gulls and Terns) of KVCR

Gulls and terns are the other two groups of migrant birds in KVCR. Gulls are large group of seabirds belonging to the family Laridae. A juvenile gull's plumage constantly morphs from varying shades of patterned browns before settling into its mature coloration - gray, white and black. During mating season, most adult seagulls change colours - head feathers commonly change to either bright white or dark brown. Gulls are resourceful, inquisitive and intelligent birds, demonstrating complex methods of communication and a highly developed social structure. As such, they exploit a variety of habitats, both coastal and inland, consume a wide variety of food, and are often extremely abundant. They are also great wanderers.

There is a great deal of diversity between different gull species, with the smallest being the Little Gull (120 g and 29 cm) and the largest being the Great Black-beaked Gull (1.75 kg and 75 cm). They are typically medium to large birds, usually grey or white, often with black markings on the head or wings. They typically have harsh wailing or squawking calls, stout, long bills, and webbed feet. Gulls are generally ground-nesting carnivores that feed on live food or scavenge opportunistically.

Maximum number of gulls moves into KVCR during the period between December and March. Among gulls, Brown-headed Gulls reach the destination prior to the arrival of other wintering gulls (Table 5).

Table 5: Mean abundance of wintering gulls observed in KVCR from September 2005 to May 2009.

Species	2005-2006		2006-2007		2007-2008		2008-2009	
	Mean	Range	Mean	Range	Mean	Range	Mean	Range
Black-headed Gull	260.3	0-700	3570	0-11500	5490.9	0-30200	2521	0-15000
Brown-headed Gull	497.0	0-1800	5711.1	0-25000	7147.4	0-39311	2460	0-10000
Pallas's Gull	99.0	0-490	981.1	0-3500	0.54	0-3	43.6	0-100
Heuglin's Gull	92.3	0-503	125	0-600	472.9	0-2601	32	0-100
Slender billed Gull	0	0	0.3	0-3	0	0	0.2	0-1

Gulls belonging to five groups *viz.* Black-headed Gull (*Larus ridibundus*), Brown-headed Gull (*L. brunnicephalus*), Heuglin's Gull (*L. heuglini*), Slender-billed Gull (*L. genei*) and Pallas's Gull (*L. ichthyaetus*) are recorded from KVCR of which about 52% are Brown-headed and 34%are Black-headed. Slender-billed Gulls were seldom documented during 2005-2009. Log transformed data reveal that all gulls except Black-headed and Brown headed have been found declining during 2008-2009.

All the five species of gulls reported from Kerala are from KVCR. High species richness of gulls in KVCR has been attributed to the availability of food and the extent of exposure of sand-beds, even during high tides, where gulls rest and preen. Even after two decades the Brown-headed Gull remains the dominant gull species in the KVCR, with their number increasing several folds in recent years. Around 20% of the bio-geographic population of Brown-headed Gull has been recorded from KVCR. A comparative study showed that Brown-headed and black-headed gulls prefer KVCR rather than the Kole wetlands as a wintering ground in the West Coast of Kerala.

Gulls in KVCR exhibit two trend patterns- an increasing pattern of scavenging gulls (Black-headed Gull and Brown-headed Gull) and a decreasing pattern of specialist gulls (Pallas's Gull and Slender-billed Gull)[140]. These trends clearly indicate that the wetland is highly exploited, may be to meet the livelihood issues of locals/neighbouring urbanites. The declining trend of specialist gulls has been attributed to the loss of potential wintering ground, pollution of water and soil, secondary poisoning, natural phenomenon such as reduction in rainfall, predation by dogs, crows and raptors, developmental activities such as construction of over bridges, land filling (of wetland) and fluctuations in the level of pH and salinity[141].

Black-headed Gull and Brown-headed Gull are the dominant species while Pallas's Gull and Slender-billed Gull are lesser in number. The numbers of Black-headed Gulls and Brown-headed Gulls have increased, while specialist gulls such as Pallas's Gull and Slender-billed Gull are stable or in decline. Increasing trend of scavenging gulls can be attributed to the solid waste dumping in various habitats of KVCR[142].

Terns, belonging to the family Sternidae have a worldwide distribution and are normally found near the sea, rivers, or wetlands. Most species of terns are declining in numbers due to human activities, including habitat degradation or loss, pollution, disturbances, and predation.

A total of ten species of terns, Caspian Tern (*Sterna caspia*), Common Tern (*S. hirundo*), Gull-billed Tern (*Gelochelidon nilotica*), Saunders's Little Tern (*S. saundersi*), River Tern (*S. aurantia*), Sandwich Tern (*S. sandvicensis*), Sooty Tern (*S. fuscata*) Large Crested Tern (*S. bergii*), Lesser Crested Tern (*S. bengalensis*) and Whiskered Tern (*Chlidonias hybridus*) are recorded from KVCR. The most abundant terns of KVCR are Little Terns and Common Terns. The least represented species is Sandwich Tern.

Over the years, the population of Common and Little Terns in KVCR has increased several folds, whereas, that of Lesser Crested, Large Crested, Whiskered and Sandwich Terns showed a drastic decline. Gull-billed Tern did not exhibit considerable change during this period. In particular, the Sandwich Tern, which was a common species during 1989 at KVCR showed a sharp decline during our study.

The Sandwich Tern is locally called "*Kadalundi ala*" (in the local language, Malayalam 'ala' means Tern) because of its high abundance in the KVCR. Unfortunately recent reports pointed out that the population of this species is showing a downward trend in KVCR. In fact, this was the triggering force that drove our interest in monitoring the population trend of this bird in KVCR. Workers on African-Eurasian migratory water birds have included the Sandwich and other Terns in their list of birds that demanded conservation initiative in their wintering and breeding grounds. We could observe that in KVCR the abundance of terns, in general, fluctuates sharply year-after-year. At the same time the number of Sandwich terns has remained low (for the past seven years), although the species has been a regular visitor on the Kannur and Manjeshwaram beaches (about 200 to 300 kms away from KVCR) in the northern part of Kerala (Table 4). Several factors can be attributed to the declining trend of terns in general. To name a few: (1) displacement by the increasing abundance of Common and Little Terns, (2) they might have shifted their foraging ground due to the non- availability of the potential prey species, (3) increased anthropogenic disturbances in this fragile estuarine environment and (4) the presence of humans, Brahminy Kites, Black Kites, House Crows, Jungle Crows, stray dogs and/ or cats.

Macrobenthic prey that influence the habitat use of shorebirds

Our study establishes that polychaetes, crustaceans and bivalved molluscs are the major invertebrate preys of migrant shorebirds. The crustaceans included small and medium-sized crabs, cosmonotous crabs, prawns and mantis shrimps (stomatopods). Apart from these, the migrant shorebirds prey on small fishes and aquatic insects. Seven categories of invertebrates have been recorded from the KVCR (Fig 3). The most abundant prey are polychaetes, followed by prawns, cosmonotous crab, small crabs medium sized crab and stomatopods (Plate 7 a, b, c, d, e).

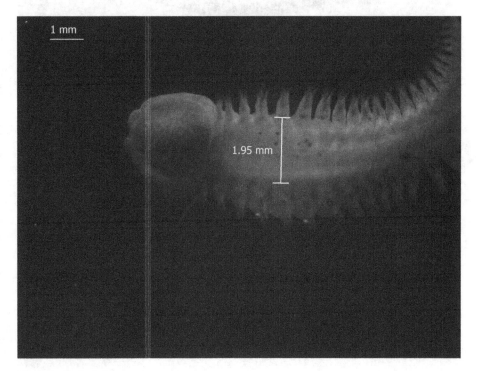

Plate 7 a: Polychaete

Plate 7 b: Cosmonotous crab

Plate 7c: Soft bivalves

Plate 7 d *Dotilla* sp. (Small crab)

Plate 7 e: Stomatopod

Fig 3-Prey species recorded during the study period (2010 to 2012) in KVCR.

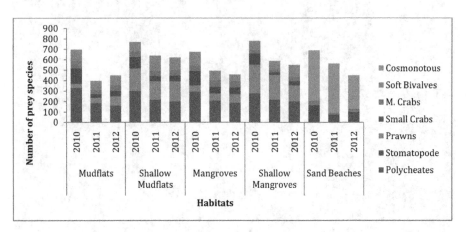

Table 6- Polychaetes recorded from different habitats

Species	Mudflats	Shallow Mudflats	Mangroves	Shallow Mangroves
Perinereis cavifrons	P	P	NP	NP
P. nuntia	P	P	P	P
Nereis chilkaensis	P	P	P	P
N. capensis	P	P	NP	NP
N. cricognatha	P	P	NP	NP
Dendroneries aestuarina	P	P	P	P
D. arborifera Peters	P	P	P	P
Ancistrosyllis constrica	P	P	P	P
Marphysagravelyi	P	P	NP	NP
M. macintoshi	NP	NP	P	P
M. stragulum	NP	NP	P	P
Glycera alba	P	P	P	P
G. longipinnis	P	P	P	P
Ceratonereis burmensis	P	P	P	P
Namalycastis sp	P	P	P	P
Heteromastus filiformis	P	P	P	P
*Loimia*sp	P	P	P	P
Tylonereisbogoyawleskyi	P	P	NP	NP
Capitellacapitata	P	P	NP	NP

P= Present; NP= Not Present

Six species of polychaetes have been recorded exclusively on mudflats and shallow mudflats and two species exclusively from mangroves and shallow mangroves and the remaining 11 species from all habitats except sand beaches (Table 6). Abundance of Polychaetes is higher in the West Coast when compared to the East Coast of India [143] and is attributed to the existence of loose texture of sediment formed as a result of the presence of sandy-silt [144, 145, 146, 143]. Polychaetes act as good indicators of organic enrichment and environmental perturbations. They are the most abundant species often comprising more than 29 % of the total number of macro-benthic species[147]. The presence of high density of polychaetes on mudflats and mangroves could be due to the presence of sea grass (fairly rich population of sea grass was observed in the study area) and optimal level of sediment granulometry; both factors could have influence on the community structure of polychaetes and other macro-benthic animals[148].

Crabs form another important group of prey for shorebirds. Thirteen species (Table 7) of crabs are documented from KVCR of which, six species are of smaller size and seven are of medium size. The highest number of smaller crabs is recorded from mangroves followed by mudflats, shallow mudflats, shallow mangroves and sand beaches.

Table 7- Distribution of Crabs in different habitats at KVCR from 2010 to 2012

S. No	Species	Mudflats	Shallow Mudflats	Mangroves	Shallow Mangroves	Sand Beaches
Small Crabs						
1	*Sesarma quadrata*	P	P	P	P	P
2	*Uca annulipes*	NP	NP	P	P	P
3	*Dotilla myctiroides*	P	P	P	P	NP
4	*Dotilla malabaricus*	P	P	P	P	NP
5	*Metapograpsus messor*	NP	NP	P	P	NP
6	*Macrophthalmus sulcatus*	P	P	P	P	NP
Medium and Large sized Crabs						
7	*Uca (Gelasimus) vocans*	P	P	P	P	P
8	*Metapograpsusmaculatus*	P	NP	NP	NP	P
9	*Ocypode ceratophthalmus*	P	NP	NP	NP	P
10	*Scylla olivcaea*	NP	P	P	P	P
11	*Uca (Thalassuca) vocans*	P	P	P	P	P
12	*Scopimera sp.*	P	NP	NP	NP	P
13	*Matutalunaris*	NP	NP	NP	NP	P

Abundance of prawns is higher in shallow mangroves followed by shallow mudflats. Five species of prawns, *Penaeus indicus, P. canaliculatus, Metapenaeus monoceros, M. dobsoni and Macrobrachium rosenbergii* are documented from KVCR. Among which *P. indicus and M. dobsoni* are the most common species at shallow water and mangroves.

One species of Cosmonotous crab and two species of mantis shrimps *(Oratosquilla gonypetes* and *Plesionika* sp) are available in the sand beach. Bivalves are very common in Kadalundi, and *Donax cuneatus* is the most common and only species of soft bivalve recorded from KVCR. The highest number of *Donax cuneatus* is recorded from shallow mudflats followed by shallow mangroves, mudflats and mangroves.

The aquatic resources provide diverse habitats for wildlife particularly waterbirds[149]. Waterbirds are considered as bio-indicators of wetland ecosystem, as they quickly respond to changes in vegetation composition and water level fluctuation[150, 151]. In order to understand the waterbird community structures and population status of existing species in their dwelling areas, the population fluctuation of waterbirds in wetland habitats needs to be determined[152].

Macro-invertebrates are integral components of aquatic ecosystems and they maintain various levels of interactions between community and environment[153]. Macrobenthic animals play a vital role in the circulation and recycling of nutrients in aquatic ecosystems by accelerating the breakdown of decaying organic matter into simpler inorganic forms[154].

Studies[143, 155] on the distribution and abundance of macrobenthic invertebrates reveal that the highest value of organic carbon is observed at Calicut region than the other regions of West Coast of India. The highest values of organic carbon and nitrogen are observed at shallow mangroves of KVCR (organic carbon 1.19 % and nitrogen 0.1991 %) followed by shallow mudflats (organic carbon 1.16 % and nitrogen 0.0992 %). Increased percentage of organic carbon and nitrogen may be major reasons for the abundance of macro-benthic prey animals.

The distribution of macrobenthic communities is highly correlated to the type of sediment in general and the organic content of the sediment in particular[156, 157, 158, 159]. In KVCR mudflats and mangroves have loose texture of sediments which are organically rich and, therefore, the abundance of macro-benthic animals is high in these regions.

It was reported in an earlier study[160] that high population density and rich biomass of polychaetes are associated with the presence of sandy substrate. Generally, water content in the sediment reflects an increase in fine particles (mud and clay) that can retain more water than coarse particles (sand and gravel). Such fine deposits or particles are commonly composed of decomposable organic constituents. As the organic content represents an important direct or indirect food source for benthic organisms, elevated organic matter may result in an enhancement of benthic metabolism [161, 162].

When the sediment texture is changed, the quantity of organic matter, nutrients, and the level of oxygen is also changed significantly. This could have led to changes in the composition and abundance of the polychaetes, because any disturbance in the soft sediment can damage the existing fauna and render the habitat available for new colonization and succession of species [163].

In Kadalundi overall population of benthic organisms especially of polychaetes and crabs shows a declining trend (Fig 3).

Relationship between shorebird count and prey abundance

Macrobenthic invertebrates constitute a major part of the diet of migratory shorebirds during their wintering period [164, 165, 166] and strongly influence the distribution [132] and feeding behaviour of[127] waterbirds. Many shorebird species prey mainly on crustaceans and polychaetes that inhabit muddy area[63]. Waterbirds acquire important nutrients by feeding on benthic macro-invertebrates, and the availability of which is influenced by physico-chemical variables such as water depth and water chemistry[167]. Salinity and acidity also affect the distribution and richness of benthic invertebrates[168, 169, 170, 171, 172,] This in turn can affect the feeding ecology of waterbirds. We strongly feel that this is a major reason that justifies the distribution of shorebirds in the West Coast especially in Kadalundi-Vallikkunnu Community Reserve. Moreover, the nutrient rich top soil plays an important role in the growth and sustenance of invertebrates in KVCR.

Research on the foraging and feeding of shorebirds at diverse locations across the globe indicate that polychaetes are one of the primary prey items chosen by shorebirds[171, 172]. In KVCR polychaete density is higher than that of other invertebrate groups. Earlier studies in KVCR showed that polychaetes and crabs are important food items of shorebirds[65] and other waterbirds[52]. Among the macrobenthic prey animals, mantis shrimps and cosmonotous crabs are available only at sand beach. During high tide the shorebirds (smaller to larger size) congregate mainly on the sand beach, forage on tidal waves and selectively pick up cosmonotous crabs, small crabs and occasionally mantis shrimps. The invertebrate rich KVCR is, therefore, considered as one of the most important stop over sites for migrant shorebirds in the West Coast of India. In Kadalundi shorebirds forage very actively during low tide, especially during the first two hours [65] probably due to the fluctuations in the availability of epifaunal and infaunal prey on the sediment. During the hot hours of the day, majority of shorebirds rest on the sand beds when the tide is low[65] then gradually start their feeding activities and in the late evening they become more active in feeding. This shows that higher the atmospheric temperature lower will be the rate of feeding.

It is a fact that preparation for, and the execution of, long distance flights among migrating birds involve many physiological changes [173, 174, 175, 176] and such changes mainly depend on the nature of food available. Majority of shorebirds prefer polychaetes followed by crabs, mantis shrimps and so on and this could be due to the proportionate decrease in the level of carbohydrates and proteins. In *Ceratonereis burmensis,* one of the most abundant polychaetes in the KVCR, the value of carbohydrates is 45.8 ±4.382 mg/gm (mean±SD) whereas, that of protein is 73.2±1.588 mg/gm (mean±SD). In *Dotilla myctiroides,* one of the dominant crab species (small sized), the value of carbohydrates is 44.3±4.211 mg/gm (mean±SD) and that of protein is 41.3±1.862 mg/gm(mean ±SD). Prawns, *Penaeus indicus,* are available at shallow water regions of mudflats and mangroves and are seen throughout the seasons, most abundantly during post monsoon. Their value of carbohydrates is 33.6±2.702 mg/gm (mean±SD) and that of protein is 57±1.225 mg/gm (mean ±SD). In mantis shrimps, *Oratosquilla gonypetes,* the value of carbohydrates is 3.64 ±1.817 mg/gm(mean ±SD) and that of protein is 53±1.871 mg/gm(mean ±SD). In *Scylla olivacea,* the most dominant medium sized crab abundant at the sand beach, the value of carbohydrates is 59.4±2.611 mg/gm (mean±SD) and that of protein is 60.2 ±457 mg/gm (mean ±SD). Cosmonotous crabs are found only on sand beach, and the value of carbohydrates is 63±2.538 mg/gm (mean±SD) and that of protein is 76.1±0.994 mg/gm (mean ±SD). The maximum amount of carbohydrates and proteins were observed in cosmonotous crabs. Usually fuel reserves are accumulated in the form of fat and protein[177]. Earlier studies [178, 179] indicated that protein rich food is essential for long migrant shorebirds to meet their energy requirements.

The significant and inverse relation between number of shorebirds and densities of polychaetes on the mangroves was probably due to sustained shorebird predation on polychaetes and resulting decline in densities of benthic invertebrates [180, 181, 182]. Environmental factors other than prey abundance also have influence on species richness and abundance of shorebirds [182]. Water depth in the foraging area is an example. It has direct influence on feeding activities of shorebirds.

During low tide (in shallow water) Lesser Sand Plover prefers a feeding depth ranging from 0 to 6 cm, Common Redshank 0 to 9 cm and Whimbrel ranging from of 0 to 14 cm. Water depth has been considered as a key environmental factor regulating the availability of food for birds in the Ghanaian lagoons[17]. All ground-feeding waterbird guilds, representing majority of waterbirds that feed in the lagoons, require shallow water (no deeper than 20 cm)[17].

Hardening of sediment is an environmental constraint for foraging shorebirds. Therefore, conservation and restoration of soft bottom intertidal habitats, such as mudflats, may be particularly critical for probing shorebirds[183].

CHAPTER FOUR

CONSERVATION ISSUES OF KVCR

Sand mining and salinity intrusion

Sand mining is a serious environmental issue in India and public awareness against illegal and uncontrolled sand mining is gaining momentum. Marine sand mining has had an impact on seabed flora and fauna as dredging and extraction of sand and gravel from the benthic (sea bottom) zone leads to a net decline in biological diversity. Many studies on the effects of dredging have reported declines in both bivalves and worms that are key prey species for many waterbirds [184, 185, 186, 187, 188]. Long term recovery can occur only where original sediment composition is being restored.

Sand mining (legal and/or illegal) has been observed (Plate 8) as a regular practice in KVCR. The rate of sand loading in boats per month has been increasing every year (Fig 4) especially during September to December, the ideal period for construction activities in Kerala. The rate of sand mining in KVCR is comparatively lesser during the rainy season (June to July). As sand mining results in disappearance of sand banks - the resting place of sea birds - the gulls have to seek out other places to rest, which can be one of the reasons for the gradual decrease in the number of gulls over the years from sand banks[141].

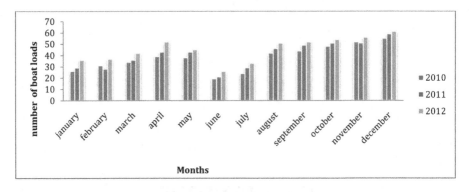

Fig 4: Sand mining from KVCR during 2010 to 2012

We hypothesized that sand mining in KVCR is one of the major environmental threats triggering the decline in the bird population, which has been proved true (Fig 1 & 2). Sand mining removes the nutrient rich soil (an ideal habitat for polychaetes, crustaceans etc.) which results in salinity intrusion. Salinity is a limiting factor in the distribution of living organisms[189]. Its variation due to dilution and/or evaporation influences the survival of fauna in the intertidal zone[190, 191]. This may be the reason for the reduction in number of polychaetes over the years in KVCR.

In the West Coast of India the abundance of diatoms is inversely proportional to salinity [192, 193, 194, 195]. Invertebrate diversity decreased dramatically above salinity of 40 ppt[196]. Furthermore, higher salinity is reported to cause reduction in the prawn and fish diversity and abundance as well[102].

A significant consequence of sand mining is that it changes the chemistry of the ecosystem[197, 198]. Studies have established that organic carbon, phosphorous, nitrogen and salinity serve as important factors that regulate the availability of polychaetes and other invertebrates[199]. Veliger, the planktonic larva of benthic molluscs and some holoplankton are particularly vulnerable to changes in water chemistry which affects the developments of their calcareous skeleton. These invertebrates serve as diet for many migrant shorebirds.

With the escalating demand for construction materials, demand for sand has gone up at an alarming rate and has culminated in the overexploitation of this precious natural resource especially of the wetland ecosystem. When large portion of wetlands is being exploited to solve the livelihood issues of local population, conservation components of the wetlands and their biodiversity are often neglected. If the non-judicious mining of sand in KVCR continues, the existence of nutrient rich mudflats will be under constant threat. Its far reaching impact will be reflected on the life of benthos directly and wintering population of migratory shorebirds indirectly. The raised sand bed on the eastern and southern sides of mudflat of KVCR normally help in preventing the intrusion of rough sea into the mudflat area and hence the important foraging ground of the birds has been protected hitherto. However, non-systematic removal of sand from the sand beds, in recent years, has resulted in deposition of sand into the nutrient rich mudflats. Systematic human intervention to keep a check on the intrusion of sand into the mudflats is needed to protect the wintering ground of many shorebirds. The sand banks in Kadalundi estuary is a roosting place for gulls and terns which forage there during the wintering periods in large flocks. Taking these facts into serious consideration, the community reserve and management committee should take up necessary actions to regulate the removal of sand by employing appropriately developed protocols. Apart from this the Government of India needs to promote salinity control related research initiatives in mangrove habitats as it is inextricably linked to the tropic marine food web too[86].

Plate 8: Sand loaded country boats

Solid waste dumping at mudflats and mangroves

Dumping of huge quantities of solid waste especially of plastics, clothes carry bags, bottles, food wrappers, domestic waste, poultry farm waste (Fig 5) and slaughter house waste especially on the mudflats and mangrove areas is a regular practice in KVCR. Apart from the primary data collected during day hours, secondary data has also been procured from people who have direct or indirect concern over the welfare of KVCR. The secondary data reveal that pickup vans and auto-rickshaws regularly bring in poultry wastes (Plate 9) to the estuary during night hours. Decaying parts of chicken in the estuary attract the house crows (Plate 10), kites, dogs and cats. Dumping of these wastes usually increase after social/communal gatherings in the neighbouring localities. The peak wintering period for migrant shorebirds in the community reserve is December-January and unfortunately coincides with the period when solid waste dumping is at its highest.

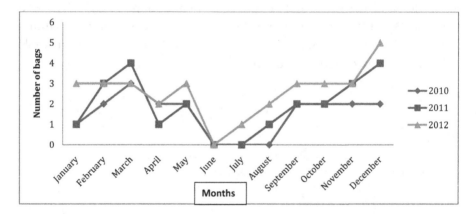

Fig 5: Poultry waste bags observed in the KVCR during 2010 to 2012

Plastics pose a serious threat, especially, to the coastal ecosystems and marine life. The plastic carry bags and plastic bottles cause considerable damage to the fragile mangrove ecosystem and its unique diversity. The carry bags are known to clog aerial roots of mangroves, resulting in poor air exchange and sometimes this may lead to the death of seedlings[78, 88]. It may also alter the strength of biological interactions that may lead to the death of fragile benthic organisms[78, 88]. As a result, prawns, crabs, benthivore fish and waterbirds that depend heavily on benthic organisms for their survival will also be severely affected [200]. Oysters and some species of mollusks usually keep their shells open during the high tide in order to collect their food[92] and the carry bags thrown into the mangroves may cover their foot/shell partially or completely and may result in asphyxiation and ultimately lead to their death[88].

When wind enters the floating plastic bottles and thin plastic carry bags, hanging over the mangrove tree branches, a peculiar sound is produced, which causes panic among the foraging migratory and resident waterbirds leading to their dispersal[88]. The foraging birds may learn to stop responding to such stimulus as they get habituated. Earlier studies pointed out that the recurrence of such events may even force the birds to leave the habitat permanently[201, 202]. Migratory waterbirds are unable to compensate the lost feeding time, which in turn affects their recouping of energy reserves and maintaining their migration accuracy[92].

Poultry waste disposal raises potassium level

Excess amount of waste deposition (especially from slaughter houses and poultry farms) increases the concentration of Potassium in water and on mudflats[203]. In KVCR, the lowest level of potassium was observed in September (8.43 mg/l) and the highest level during August (70mg/l) (Table 8). The lowest level in September may be due to the increase in freshwater inflow due to rain[204]. High concentration of potassium in water leads to eutrophication which may lead to the disruption of the food web and may be one of the reasons for the shorebird population decline.

Table 8- The level of Potassium (mg/l) in the KVCR during January 2010 to December 2012:

Months	2010	2011	2012
January	10.78	11.27	40.00
February	11.23	12.78	29.00
March	11.01	13.24	41.00
April	10.27	11.67	56.00
May	10.03	11.11	52.65
June	9.89	10.78	2180
July	9.04	10.35	20.10
August	8.78	9.24	70.00
September	8.43	10.76	16.20
October	8.97	10.98	24.50
November	9.45	11.78	35.00
December	10.34	12.45	37.50

Plate 9: Poultry waste in jute bags – a common scene in KVCR

Plate 10: Crows attracted by poultry waste in KVCR

Changes in environmental variables

The analyses of physical and chemical parameters indicate that humidity was found to fluctuate whereas, air and water temperature, salinity, pH, PO_4^{2-}, Ca^{2+}, K^+ and Mg^+ were found to increase significantly and at the same time NO_3^- was found to decline. Changes in the above mentioned parameters except Ca^{2+} and K^+ were gradual.

In KVCR bird abundance decreases with increase in air temperature. The foraging behaviour of Lesser Sand Plover[65] is significantly influenced by air temperature. Increase in temperature is directly proportional to foraging attempt rate, but inversely proportional to success rate in foraging[183]. The temperature is known to have a significant effect on the activity rates and the availability of the prey items of shorebirds also[205]. There is a significant relationship between maximum temperature and foraging effort in the Bar-tailed Godwit and the Lesser Knot.

Water pH of wetland has a profound influence on the population characteristics of birds[7]. For example, acidic wetlands are inferior waterfowl habitats[206]. A significant relationship between waders' diversity and pH of the wetland habitats was established through scientific studies[99, 207, 208].

Increase in pH in the KVCR may be a result of the changes in the chemistry of the habitat due to solid waste dumping and/or sand mining. Studies made in Cochin estuary[209] and other areas[210] identified pH as the best variable and is highly correlated with the macrobenthic faunal assemblages.

The concentration of nitrates and phosphates significantly influences the density of shorebirds. This might be due to the limiting effects of these nutrients on the productivity in the ecosystem and the consequent faunal distribution and abundance [208, 211, 192, 212, 213, 214, 99].

Nitrates have a decreasing trend and phosphates have an increasing trend in KVCR [139] High nutrient loading in coastal ecosystems causes serious eutrophication problems[215]. In an eutrophic shallow environment, oxygen-depleted water gets generated occasionally at the bottom of water column due to the accumulation of organic matter [216, 217] and can cause death of benthic macrofauna [218].

To conclude, the physico-chemical characteristics of water and sediment largely determine the waterbird community of aquatic habitats. This is primarily by their direct or indirect impact on the availability and abundance of birds' prey. The role of food abundance on waterbird densities has been well established [219, 220, 221, 222, 223, 224, 127, 225, 226, 227, 99]. The declining trends of migrant shorebirds at KVCR may be due to the declining trends in the abundance of benthos across the habitats[148]. The abundance of macrobenthic fauna was significantly related to certain important parameters like nitrates, organic carbon etc[139]. The relation between the prey abundance and the shorebird abundance, and the relation of physico-chemical parameters to prey abundance and shorebirds abundance have been established in KVCR through scientific studies and it substantiate similar studies.

Tourists

Tourists visiting KVCR spend their time sitting on the highway bridge adjacent to the resting and feeding ground of gulls and terns[142] and occasionally throw stones on the flocks to capture the spectacular image of the flying birds. Such disturbances serve as deterrence to the birds from congregating at the same spot. As the tourism potential of the coastal wetland habitats of Kerala is soaring, the influx of tourists to these areas will pose a threat to the migratory shorebirds unless thoughtful management measures or conservation strategies are adopted/ implemented.

Shorebirds react to the presence of nearby humans in various ways. Depending on the proximity and type of human activity (walking, running, fishing, dog exercising), shorebirds may respond either by spending more time watching the potential human threat [228, 68, 229], by walking away from approaching humans [229], or by flying to nearby undisturbed section of beach[230]. Although these types of reactions have some effect on shorebirds, particularly a reduction in foraging time, a potentially more serious consequence of anthropogenic activity would be the abandoning of a potential foraging area by some or all shorebirds.

Domestic Cats, Dogs, Kites, Crows and humans

Cats and dogs usually visit sand beaches to feed on the fishes, crabs, prawns etc. discarded by the fishing boats and their mere presence scares the shorebirds [142] away from their foraging grounds. Fishermen and other local people engaged in the collection of bivalves are also creating inconveniences to the foraging shorebirds.

In the presence of human beings, the birds alter their feeding behaviour[229, 231]. The extent of this behavioural change vary from subtle decline in swallow rates [232] to more drastic changes such as permanent avoidance of an entire estuary[233]. Predation risk is an important factor in habitat selection of birds[234, 235]. The abundance of raptors also has an influence on the shorebirds' habitat selection [236, 237]. In KVCR, the Kites and Crows are attracted to the solid organic waste being deposited at the foraging ground from poultry and slaughter houses and cause considerable disturbances to the active feeding and the maintenance of flock composition of shorebirds[41]. Larger flocks are more easily disturbed[238, 239, 240, 241, 242].

Mobile phone towers

After the erection of mobile phone towers, one on either side of KVCR, gulls and terns were found to shift to nearby areas for foraging. A significant decline has also been noted in the number of migrants. The mobile radiation may be one of the reasons[244, 245, 246, 247, 248, 249, 243] for the decline in shorebird population. Detailed studies need to be undertaken to establish this.

Incursion of mangroves

In KVCR mudflats and mangroves are closely situated unique ecosystems. Within the past several years the mangroves in KVCR has been slowly proliferating over the mudflats, the primary foraging ground of migratory shorebirds[65]. This incursion has resulted in reduction in the area of open mudflats available for foraging. In recent years mangrove saplings have been planted on intertidal flats as a part of expanding the total area of mangrove forests in India. Mangrove forest is very important to coastal ecosystem sustenance and community security; same is the case of neighbouring habitats. Therefore, ecosystem services of neighbouring habitats also need to be considered seriously while identifying sites for restoration of mangroves. The major impact of the conversion of a tidal mudflat system into a mangrove forest system would involve transformation of both the hydrological regime and biotic communities. These changes included decreased flow velocity[250], replacement of shorebirds and waterfowl with tree-dwelling egrets, diminished benthic diatom production relative to mangrove litter and changes in benthic dominancy from polychaetes and amphipods to crabs[251].

Sediment quality

In KVCR the proportion of clay, silt and coarse and fine sand vary with habitats. The highest content of clay and silt was observed in shallow mudflats followed by shallow mangroves, mudflats and mangroves and the lowest value in the sand beach. Sand beaches had the highest amount of fine sand, followed by mangroves, mudflats shallow mangroves, and shallow mudflats. In the case of coarse sand, the highest value was at mangroves, then at shallow mudflats and shallow mangroves followed by mudflats and sand beaches. Mangrove sediment is rich in fine sand followed by coarse sand, silt and clay.

The sediment quality is one of the vital factors controlling the benthic life[252, 253, 210]. The organic matter in surface sediments is an important source of food for benthic fauna [254, 156, 255, 256, 257, 159, 258]. The grain size and organic content of soil define distinct species assemblages. Distribution of macro-benthos could be explained by the classification of physical characteristics of sediment in tidal flats[259]. The main environmental factors that influence the distribution of macrobenthic animals are organic matter, salinity and sediment characteristics, especially mud or clay content [252, 260, 143, 210]. The changes in benthic species composition and abundances are often linked to the interaction of fine sediments, organic material, and chemical contaminants.

The sediment hardness is an environmental constraint for shorebirds like dunlin and, therefore, conservation and restoration of soft bottom intertidal habitats, such as mudflats, may be particularly critical for probing shorebirds[183]. Any structural modification of soft sediment in the feeding mudflats due to compaction of sediments, dumping of debris or other reasons will reduce the substrate penetrability. Such a situation may inhibit successful foraging and may be detrimental to the shorebirds[242]. Environmental inputs, such as nutrients and pollutants, can lead to the appearance of different types of prey as well as different feeding conditions which often affect prey biomass and availability [261, 262, 263].

Increase in the height of sand bed and reduction in the area of mudflats

For the past ten years, sand beds in KVCR have been expanding gradually which in turn results in a gradual reduction in the area covered by mudflats, (Plate 11). In the year 2012 - 2013 the total area of mudflats was eight hectares and is now shrinking rapidly, which in turn resulted in the decline in the number of visiting shorebirds.

Plate 11:

Decrease in the depth of mudflats – a constraint to shorebirds

The depth of mudflats has been gradually decreasing over the years which indicates a gradual hardening of sloppy mud. The depth of mudflats was measured three times during the first week of January, June and September mainly on the basis of congregation of migrant shorebirds for foraging. During 1980's the depth of mudflats was more than six feet, when the local community had been actively engaged in coconut husk retting, for coir industry, on the mudflats. In January, 2010 the average depth was 54.11cm, and in 2011 it was 45.22 cm. It came down to 38.16 cm in 2012, 31.22 in 2013 and in September

2014 it was 29.29. If it goes down at the same pace, the survival of living beings in the mudflat will be jeopardized.

Stoppage of husk retting

Retting of coconut husk is the basic process involved in the production of coir and coir goods and is one of the most popular traditional occupations in the coastal areas of Kerala. In KVCR, 50% of exposed mudflats, out of eight hectares in the estuary, usually get exposed during low tide. This area was used as a regular husk retting ground during 1980's. Eventhough the process of husk retting in KVCR had been discontinued during early 1990s, the remains of the decayed/decomposed husk (being buried till the end of 1980s) are still discernible in the area close to the mudflats and mangroves (Plate 12).

Earlier studies revealed that husk retting is detrimental to the environment as the pH of the surrounding water comes down from neutral to the acidic and BOD (Biological Oxygen Demand) level goes up with the progress of retting. This may lead to the deterioration in the water quality, which in turn becomes detrimental to the aquatic life. The continued and intensive exploitation of wetlands for husk retting has deleterious effect on the fishery resources.

In KVCR polychaetes and crabs are important food items of shorebirds[65, 178, 172] and other waterbirds. Among the benthic community, polychaetes are reported to dominate the retting zone followed by mollusks. Few species of polychaetes, namely *Paraheteromastus tenius*, *Perinereis cavifrons* and *Prinospio polybranchiata* were abundant in the retting zone[264] in KVCR and *Pereneries cavfrons* was the most dominant species among them. These species were getting benefitted from the retting zone. However, these species were not recorded during our study in KVCR. At present 19 species of polychaetes are documented of which the most common species are *Ceratonereis burmensis* Monoro, *Namalycastis sp.*, *Heteromastus filiformis* and these species were not recorded during earlier studies[264]. This change in the diversity of polychaete may be due to husk retting process.

Plate 12: Decayed/decomposed coconut husk in the area close to mangrove and mudflat

Recommendations for conservation and management of habitats of migrant waterbirds visiting India in general and KVCR in particular:

1. A Centre to promote in-depth study and training on bird migration should be established in the West Coast of India and this Centre should focus on studies on the status of migrant shorebirds in the Central Asian Flyway with special reference to Indian sub-continent.

2. This Centre should take initiative to identify the conservation issues of migrant shorebirds at their wintering/summering grounds in India and submit the findings as recommendations to the policy makers through the regional/local self- government bodies.

3. Dialogues should be initiated between the Department/s of Forest and Wildlife (of States in the traditional passage sites of Central Asian Flyway in India) and the stakeholders (that include local communities, conservationists, academic communities in the neighboring institutions etc.) as a confidence building measure.

4. The Centre should organize regular public awareness creation programmes with the support of NGOs/local academic institutions/clubs etc. on the significance of conservation of shorebirds and their habitats.

5. Efforts should be initiated to make a thorough attitudinal change among the local public especially on solid waste management.

6. Steps need to be taken for KVCR to be declared as 'Important Bird Area' with immediate effect.

7. Continuous and systematic monitoring of both migrant and resident species of birds in the KVCR should be done.

8. A watch tower needs to be erected for continuous monitoring of the KVCR to manage anthropogenic conservation threats.

9. Local people of Kadalundi need to be made aware of the judicious management of estuarine resources.

10. Conventional method of fishing should be promoted in the estuary of KVCR.

REFERENCES

1. Birdlife International (2012) Species factsheet: Great Knot. http://www.birdlife.org

2. Balachandran, S. (2006) The decline in wader populations along the east coast of India with special reference to Point Calimere, south-east India. *Waterbirds around the world.* Eds. G.C. Boere CA Galbraith DA Stroud. The Stationery Office, Edinburgh, UK. 296-301pp.

3. Kannan, V., & J. Pandiyan (2012) Shorebirds (Charadriidae) of Pulicat Lake, India with special reference to conservation. *World Journal of Zoology* 7 (3): 178-191.

4. Mundkur, T. (2006) Flyway conservation in the Central Asian Flyway. Workshop Introduction. In: Boere G.C., Galbraith C.A., Stroud D.A. (eds). Waterbirds around the world. The Stationery Office, Edinburgh, UK. 263p.

5. Pyrovetsi, M., & E. Papastergiadou (1992) Biological conservation implications of water-level fluctuations in a wetland of International Importance: Lake Kerkini, Macedonia, Greece. *Environment Conservation* 19: 235–244.

6. Sandilyan, S., Thiyagesan, K., & R. Nagarajan (2010a) Major decline in species-richness of waterbirds in the Pichavaram mangrove wetlands, southern India. *Wader Study Group Bulletin* 117 (2): 91–98.

7. Manikannan, R., Asokan, S., & A.S.M. Ali (2012) Abundance and Factors Affecting Population Characteristics of Waders in Great Vedaranyam Swamp of Point Calimere Wildlife Sanctuary, South-east Coast of India. *International Journal of ecosystem* 2 (1): 6-14.

8. USFWS (2011) The Migratory Bird Program – Conserving America's Birds. Accessed on 20 September (2011) http://www.fws.gov/migratorybirds/

9. Skagen, K.S., & F.L. Knopf (1993) Toward Conservation of Midcontinental Shorebird Migrations. *USDA National Wildlife Research* Center-Staff Publications. Paper 646. http://digitalcommons.unl.edu/icwdm_usdanwrc/646.

10. Stroud, D.A., Baker, A., Blanco, D.E., Davidson, N.C., Delany, S., Ganter, B., Gill, R., González, P., Haanstra, L., Morrison, R.I.G., Piersma, T., Scott, D.A., Thorup, O., West, R., Wilson, J., & C. Zöckler (2006) The conservation and population status of the world's waders at the turn of the millennium. *Waterbirds around the world.* Eds. G.C. Boere, C.A. Galbraith & D.A. Stroud. The Stationery Office, Edinburgh, UK. Pp.643-648.

11. Millenium Ecosystem Assessment (2005) Ecosystems and human well-being: wetlands & water synthesis. *World resources Institute*, Washington, D.C. 68p.

12. Goss-Custard, J. D., & S. E. A. Le V. Dit Durell (1984) Feeding ecology, winter mortality and the population dynamics of Oystercatchers on the Exe estuary, *In* J. Burger, and B. L. Olla, eds., Shorebirds: migration and foraging behaviour, Pp. 190-208. New York, Plenum Press.

13. Tuckwell, J., & E. Nol (1997) Foraging behaviour of American oystercatchers in response to declining prey densities. *Canadian Journal of Zoology* 75: 170-181.

14. Backwell, P. R. Y., O'Hara, P. D., & J. H. Christy (1998) Prey availability and selective foraging in shorebirds. *Animal Behaviour* 55: 1659-1667.

15. Sutherland, T.F., Shepherd, P.C.F., & R.W. Elner (2000) Predation on meiofaunal and macrofaunal invertebrates by western sandpipers: Evidence for dual foraging modes. *Marine Biology (Berlin)* 137: 983-993.

16. Smith, P. (1991) *The Biology and management of Waders in NSW.* NPWS, Hurstville.

17. Ntiamoa-Baidu, N. Y., Piersma, T., Wiersma, R., Poot, M.M., Battley, P., & C. Gordon (1998) Habitat selection, daily foraging routines and diet of waterbirds in Coastal lagoons in Ghana. *Ibis* 140: 89-103.

18. Kalejta, B., & P.A.R. Hockey (1994) Distribution of shorebirds at the Berg River estuary, South Africa, in relation to foraging mode, food supply and environmental features. *The Ibis* 136: 233-239.

19. Zwarts, L. (1990) Increased prey availability drives pre-migration hyperphagia in Whimbrels and allows them to leave the Bane d' Arguin, Mauritania in time. *Ardea* 78: 279-300.

20. Thomas, G.H., Lanctot, R.B., & T. Szekely (2006a) Can intrinsic factors explain population declines in North American breeding shorebirds? A comparative analysis. *Animal Conservation* 9: 252–258.

21. I.W.S.G. (2003) Waders are declining worldwide: Conclusions from the 2003 International Wader Study Group Conference, Cadiz, Spain. *Wader Study Group Bull.* 101-102: 8–12.

22. Balachandran, S. (1995) Shore birds of the Marine National Park in the Gulf of Mannar, Tamil Nadu. *Journal of Bombay Natural History Society* 92: 303-311.

23. Sampath, K., & K. Krishnamurthy (1989) Shorebirds of the salt ponds at the Great Vedaranyam Salt Swamps, Tamil Nadu, India. *Stilt* 15: 20-23.

24. Sampath, K., & K. Krishnamurthy (1990) Shorebirds of the Pichavaram mangroves, Tamil Nadu, India. *Wader Study Group Bulletin* 58: 24-27.

25. Hussian, S.A., Mohapatra, K.K., & S. Ali (1984) Avifauna profile of Chilika Lake. A case for conservation. Technical Report (4), *Journal of Bombay Natural History Society.*

26. Goes, J. I., Gomes, H., Kumar, A., Gouveia, A. D., Devassy, V. P., Parulekar, A. H., & L.V.G. Rao (1992) Satellite and ship studies of phytoplankton along the west coast of India. In B. N. Desai *Oceanography of the Indian Ocean* (67–80 pp). New Delhi: Oxford & IBH.

27. Davidson, N.C. (2003) Status of wader populations on the Central/South Asian flyway. *Wader Study Group Bulletin* 101-102: 14-15.

28. Sivaperuman, C., & E.A. Jayson (2012) Population fluctuations of shorebirds in the Kole wetlands, Kerala, India. *Journal of Annals of forestry* 20 (1): 129-144.

29. Rangnekar, P. (2004) Catalogue of Birds of Goa. Dept. of Science, Technology and Environment, Govt. of Goa, Saligoa, Goa.

30. Narwade, S., & M.M. Fartade (2011) Birds of Osmanabad District of Maharashtra, India. *Journal of Threatened Taxa* 3 (2): 1567-1576.

31. Narayanan, S.P., Thomas A.P., & B. Sreekumar (2011) Ornithofauna and its conservation in the Kuttanad wetlands, southern portion of Vembanad-Kole Ramsar site, India. *Journal of Threatened Taxa* 3 (4): 1663-1676.

32. Joshi, S.P. (2012) An annotated checklist of aquatic avifauna of Rajura, Godada and Dhanora lakes of Buldhana district of Maharashtra, India. *Science Research Reporter* 2 (1): 30-33.

33. Parekh, H., & I.R. Gadhvi (2013) Waterbird diversity at Kumbharvada Marshland, Bhavnagar, Gujarath. *Life Science leaflet* 10: 53-59.

34. Pandiyan, J., Asokan, S., Thiyegesan, K. & R. Nagarajan (2006) Use of tidal flats in the Cauvery Delta region of SE India by shorebirds, gulls and terns. *Wader Study Group Bulletin* 109: 95–101.

35. Manakadan, R., & A. Pittie (2001) Standardized common and scientific names of the birds of the Indian Subcontinent. *Buceros* 6 (1): 1–37.

36. Butchart, Stuart H M, Walpole, Matt, Collen, Ben, van Strien, Arco, Scharlemann, Jörn P W, Almond, Rosamunde E A, Baillie, Jonathan E M, Bomhard, Bastian, Brown, Claire, Bruno, John, Carpenter, Kent E,

Carr, Geneviève M, Chanson, Janice, Chenery, Anna M, Csirke, Jorge, Davidson, Nick C, Dentener, Frank, Foster, Matt, Galli, Alessandro, Galloway, James N, Genovesi, Piero, Gregory, Richard D, Hockings, Marc, Kapos, Valerie, Lamarque, Jean-Francois, Leverington, Fiona, Loh, Jonathan, McGeoch, Melodie A, McRae, Louise, Minasyan, Anahit, Hernández Morcillo, Monica, Oldfield, Thomasina E E, Pauly, Daniel, Quader, Suhel, Revenga, Carmen, Sauer, John R, Skolnik, Benjamin, Spear, Dian, Stanwell-Smith, Damon, Stuart, Simon N, Symes, Andy, Tierney, Megan, Tyrrell, Tristan D, Vié, J-C., & R. Watson (2010) *Global biodiversity: indicators of recent declines. Science* 328 (5982): 1164-1168.

37. Dawson, T.P., Jackson, S.T., House, J.I., Prentice, I.C., & G.M. Mace (2011) Beyond predictions biodiversity conservation in a changing climate. *Science* 332: 53–59.

38. Zockler, C., Delany, S., & W. Hagemeijer (2003) Wader populations are declining – how will we elucidate the reasons? *Wader Study Group Bulletin* 100: 202-211.

39. Peirsma, T., & A. Lindstrom (2004) Migrating shorebirds as integrative sentinels of global environmental change. *Ibis* 146: 61–69.

40. Uthaman, P.K., & L. Namasivayan (1991) The birdlife of Kadalundi Sanctuary and its conservation. *Proceeding of Kerala Science Congress Kozhikode* Pp.37–39.

41. Aarif, K.M. (2008) Intervention of the House Crow on Migratory Shorebirds in Kadalundi Estuary. *Biosystamatica* 2 (1): 81-83.

42. Kanagavel, A., R. Pandya, C., Sinclair, A., Prithvi, & R., Raghavan. (2013) Community and conservation reserves in southern India: status, challenges and opportunities. *Journal of Threatened Taxa* 5(17): 5256–5265.

43. MoEF, The Wildlife Amendment (Protection) Act 2002. (2010b) MoEF, New Delhi. Available from http://www.envfor.nic.in/legis/wildlife/wild_act_02.htm (accessed 18 February 2014).

44. MoEF (Ministry of Environment and Forest) (2010a) The Wildlife Amendment (Protection) Act 2006 MoEF, New Delhi. http;//www.fra.org.in/law/wlact.pdf (accessed 18 February 2014)

45. Radhakrishnan, C., Gopi, K.C., & M.J. Palot (2006) *Occasional paper No 246 Records of Zoological Survey of India. Mangroves and their faunal associates in Kerala.* Zoological Survey of India, Calicut, Kerala. 81p.

46. KVCR Management Plan (2010). Kerala Forest Department, Kozhikode. 69 pp

47. Marchant, S., & P.J. Higgins (1993) Handbook of Australian, New Zealand and Antarctic birds. Vol. 2, raptors to lapwings. Melbourne: Oxford University Press.

48. Higgins, P.J., & S.J.F. Davies (1996) Handbook of Australian, New Zealand and Antarctic Birds. Volume 3: Snipe to Pigeons. *Oxford University Press*, Melbourne.

49. Barter, M.A. (2005) Yellow Sea - driven priorities for Australian shorebird researchers. Pp.158–160. *In*: Straw, P (Ed.) Status and Conservation of Shorebirds in the East Asian – Australasian Flyway. Proceedings of the Australasian Shorebird Conference, 13–15 December 2003, Canberra, Australia. International Wader Studies 17. Sydney, Australia.

50. Moores, N., Rogers, D., Kim, R-H., Hassell, C., Gosbell, K., Kim, S-A., & M-N. Park (2008) Busan. http://www.birdskorea.org/Habitats/Wetlands/Saeman geum/Downloads/Birds-Korea-SSMP-Report-2006-2008.pdf

51. McNeil, R., Diaz, M.T., & A. Villeneuve (1994) The mystery of shorebird over-summering: a new hypothesis. *Ardea* 82: 143-152.

52. Kurup, D.N. (1991a) Ecology of the birds of Malabar Coast and Lakshadweep. *Ph.D. Dissertation*, University of Calicut, Calicut. 262p.

53. Chowdhury, S.U. (2012) A survey of over-summering shorebirds at Sonadia Island, Cox's Bazar, Bangladesh. *Stilt* 61: 34-36.

54. Johnson, O.W. (1973) Reproductive condition and other features of shorebirds resident at Eniwetok Atoll during the boreal summer. *Condor* 75: 336-343.

55. Johnson, O.W. (1979) Biology of shorebirds summering on Enewetak Atoll. *Study in Avian Biology* 2: 193-205.

56. Elliott, C.C.H., Waltner, M., Underhill, L.G., Pringle, J.S., & W.J.A. Dick (1976) The migration system of the Curlew Sandpiper in Africa. *Ostrich* 47: 191-213.

57. Summers, R.W., Underhill, L.G., Waltner, M., & D.A. Whitelaw (1987) Population, biometrics and movements of the Sanderling in southern Africa. *Ostrich* 58: 24-39.

58. Summers, R.W., Underhill, L.G., & R.P. Jones (1995) Why do young waders in southern Africa delay their first return migration to the breeding grounds? *Ardea* 83: 351-357.

59. Myers, J.P. (1981) A test of three hypotheses for latitudinal segregation of the sexes in wintering birds. *Canadian Journal of Zoology* 59: 1527-1534.

60. Pienkowski, M.W., & P.R. Evans (1985) The role of migration in the population dynamics of birds. In: Sibly, R.M. and Smith, R.H. (Eds.). *Behavioural Ecology*. 331-352. Blackwell.

61. Nayak, A.K. (2006) Status of migratory shorebirds at Bhitarkanika and Chilika wetlands on the east coast of India. Waterbirds around the world. Eds. G.C. Boere, C.A. Galbraith & D.A. Stroud. The Stationery Office, Edinburgh, UK. Pp.305-307.

62. Goss-Custard, J.D., & N. Verboven (1993) Disturbance and feeding Shorebirds on the Exe estuary. *Wader Study Group Bulletin* 68: 59-66.

63. Davidson, N.C., Townshend, D.J., Pienkowski, M.W., & J.R. Speakman (1986) Why do Curlews have decurved bills? *Journal of Bird Study* 33: 63-69.

64. Burger, J., Howe, M.A., Hahn, D.C., & J. Chase (1977) Effects of tide cycles on habitat selection and habitat partitioning by migrating shorebirds. *Auk* 94: 743–758.

65. Aarif, K.M. (2009) Some Aspects of Feeding Ecology of the Lesser Sand Plover in three different zones in the Kadalundi Estuary, Kerala, South India. *Podoces* 4 (2): 100–107.

66. Aarif, K.M., Prasadan, P.K., & S. Babu (2011) Conservation significance of the Kadalundi-Vallikkunnu Community Reserve. *Current Science* 101 (6): 717-718.

67. Ehlert, W. (1964) Zur O kologie und Biologie der Erna¨hrung einiger Limikolen-Arten. *Journal of Ornithology* 105: 1–53.

68. Burger, J. (1984) Shorebirds as marine animals 17-81. International Journal of Burger and B. L. Olla [eds.], Behavior of marine animals, vol. 5: Shorebirds: breeding behavior and populations. Plenum Press, New York.

69. Zou, F.S., Yang, Q.F., Dahmer, T., Cai, J.X., & W. Zhang (2006) Habitat use of waterbirds in coastal wetland on Leizhou Peninsular, China. *Waterbirds* 29: 459–464.

70. Ali, S., & S.D. Ripley (1983) Handbook of the Birds of India and Pakistan together with those of Bangladesh, Nepal, Bhutan and Ceylon. Second edition. Oxford University Press.

71. Bryant, D.M. (1979) Effects of prey density and site character on estuary usage by overwintering waders (Charadrii). *Estuary Coast and Marine Science* 9: 369-384.

72. Goss-Custard, J.D., Warwick, R.M., Kirby, R., McGrorty, S., Clarke, R.T., Pearson, B., Rispin, W.E., Le V. dit Durell, S.E.A., & R.J. Rose (1991) Towards predicting wading bird densities from predicted prey densities in a post-barrage Severn Estuary. *Journal of Applied Ecology* 28: 1004-1026.

73. Yates, M. G., Goss-Custard, J. D., Mcgrorty, S., Lakhani, K. H., Durell, S. E. A. L. D., Clarke, R. T., Rispin, W. E., Moy, I., Yates, T., Plant, R.

A., & A. J. Frost (1993) Sediment Characteristics, Invertebrate Densities and Shorebird Densities on the Inner Banks of the Wash. *Journal of Applied Ecology* 30 (4): 599-614.

74. Rehfisch, M.M., Austin, G.E., Clark, N.A., Clarke, R.T., Holloway, S.J., Yates, M.G., Le V. dit Durrell, S.E.A., Eastwood, J.A., Goss-Custard, J.D., Swetnam, R.D. & J.R. West (2000) Predicting densities of wintering Redshank from estuary characteristics: a method for assessing the likely impacts of habitat change. *Acta Ornithologica* 35:25-32

75. Ysebaert, T., Meininger, P.L., Meire, P., Devos, K., Berrevoets, C.M., Strucker, R.C.W., & E. Kuijken (2000) Waterbird communities along the estuarine salinity gradient of the Schelde Estuary – NW Europe. *Biodiversity and Conservation* 9: 1275-1296.

76. Lourenco, P.M., Granadeiro, J.P., & J.M. Palmeirim (2005) Importance of drainage channels for waders foraging on tidal flats: relevance for the management of estuarine wetlands. *Journal of Applied Ecology* 42: 477-486.

77. Mouritsen, K.N., & K.T. Jensen (1992) Choice of microhabitat in tactile foraging dunlins *Calidris alpina*: the importance of sediment penetrability. *Marine Ecology Progress Series* 85: 1–8.

78. Lewis, L.J., & T.C. Kelly (2001) A short-term study of the effects of algal mats on the distribution and behavioural ecology of estuarine birds. *Bird Study* 48: 354-360.

79. Sandilyan S & Kathiresan K (2015). Density of waterbirds in relation to habitats of Pichavaram mangroves, Southern India 19 (2) 131-139.

80. Meltofte, H., Blew, J., Frikke, J., Rosner, H.U., & C.J. Smit (1994) Numbers and distribution of waterbirds in the Wadden Sea: results and evaluation of 36 simultaneous counts in the Dutch–German– Danish Wadden Sea 1980–1991. *Wader Study Group Bulletin* 34: 74.

81. Stroud, D.A., Chambers, D., Cook, S., Buxton, N., Fraser, B., Clement, P., Lewis, P., McLean, I, Baker, H., & S. Whitehead (2001) The UK SPA Network: Its Scope and Content Volume 1. JNCC, Peterborough.

82. Rehfisch, M.M., Holloway, S.J., & G.E. Austin (2003a) Population estimates of waders on the non-estuarine coasts of the UK and the Isle of Man during the winter of 1997–98. *Bird Study* 50: 22–32.

83. Rehfisch, M.M., Austin, G.E., Armitage, M., Atkinson, P., Holloway, S.J., Musgrove, A.J., & M.S. Pollit (2003b) Numbers of wintering waterbirds in Great Britain and the Isle of Man (1994/1995–1998/99). II Coastalwaders (Charadrii). *Biological Conservation* 112: 329–341.

84. Blew, J., Gunther K., & P. Su dbeck (2005) Bestandsentwicklun der im deutschen Wattenmeer rastenden Wat-und Wasservo¨gel von 1987/1988 bis 2001/2002. *Vogelwelt* 125: 99–125.

85. Iwamatsu, S., Suzuki, A., & M. Sato (2007) Nereidid Polychaetes as the Major Diet of Migratory Shorebirds on the Estuarine Tidal Flats at Fujimae-Higata in Japan. *Journal of Zoological Science* 24: 676-685.

86. Sato, M., & A. Nakashima (2003) A review of Asian *Hediste* species complex (Nereididae, Polychaeta) with descriptions of two new species and a re-description of *Hediste japonica* (Izuka, 1908). *Zoology Journal of Linnan Society* 137: 403–445.

87. Altenburg, W., & T.V. Spanje (1989) Utilization of mangroves by birds in Guinea-Bissau. *Ardea* 77: 1-18.

88. Sandilyan, S., & K. Kathiresan (2012a) Plastics- a formidable threat to unique biodiversity of pichavaram mangroves. *Current Science* 103 (11): 1262-1263.

89. Straw, P., & N. Saintilan (2006) Loss of shorebird habitat as a result of mangrove incursion due to sea-level rise and urbanization. *Waterbirds around the world.*E ds. G.C. Boere, C.A. Galbraith & D.A. Stroud. The Stationery Office, Edinburgh, UK. Pp. 717-720.

90. Sandilyan, S. (2009) Habitat quality and water bird utilization pattern of pichavaram wetlands southern India, *Ph.D thesis* Bharathidasan University, Thiruchirappalli, India.

91. Sandilyan, S. (2011) A scanty report on migratory waterbirds of Indian mangroves-the main bug bear: In Bhupathy S *et al.* (eds) *status of Indian birds and their conservation* SACON, Coimbatore, Pp.252-253.

92. Sandilyan, S., & K. Kathiresan (2012b) Mangrove conservation: a global perspective. *Biodiversity Conservation* 21: 3523-3542.

93. Banerjee, L.K., & D. Gosh (1998) Species diversity and distribution of mangroves in India, In: An Anthology of Indian Mangroves ENVIS Publication. Annamalai University 20 – 24.

94. Sridhar, K.R. (2004) Mangrove fungi in India.*C urrent. Science* 86: 1586-1587.

95. Hicks, G.R.F. (1984) Spatio-temporal dynamics of a meobenthic copepod and the impact of predation disturbance. *Journal of Experimental Marine Biology and Ecology* 81: 47-72.

96. Walters, K. (1988) Diel vertical migration of sediment-associated meofauna in subtropical sand and sea grass habitats. *Journal of Experimental Marine Biology and Ecology* 117: 169-186.

97. Webb, D.G. (1991) Effect of Predation by juvenile pacific salmon on marine harpacticoid copepods II. Predator density manipulation experiments. *Marine Ecology Progress Series* 72: 37-47.

98. Nagarajan, R. (1990) Factors influencing wader population in the wetland of Pichvaram Tamil Nadu, Southern India, *MPhil thesis, Bharathidasan University*, Thiruchirappalli.

99. Nagarajan, R. & K. Thiyagesan (1996) Waterbirds and substrate quality of Pichavaram wetlands, Southern India. *Ibis* 138: 710-721.

100. Sandilyan, S. (2007) Mangrove - The evergreen emerald forest. *Eco News* 13: 21.

101. Kathiresan, K. (2000) A review of studies on Pichavaram mangrove, southeast India.

Kathiresan, K., In *UNU–INWEH– UNESCO* (2004) *International Training Course on Coastal Biodiversity in Mangrove- Ecosystem Course Manual* (eds Kathiresan, K. and Jmalkhah, S. A.), CAS in Marine Biology, Annamalai University, Parangipettai, 76–89 pp.

102. Ramachandran, P.V., Lulter, G., & C. Adolph (1965) An ecological study of some pools near Mandabam (South India) formed as a result of the cyclone and tidal wave of 1964. *Journal of Marine Biological Association India* 7: 420-439.

103. Sumathi, T., Nagarajan, R., & K. Thiyagesan (2008) Effect of water depth and salinity on the population of Greater Flamingo in Point Calimere Wildlife and Bird Sanctuary, Tamilnadu, Southern India. *Scientific Transactions in Environment and Technovation* 2(1): 9-17.

104. Recher, H.F. (1966) Some aspects of the ecology of migrant shorebirds. *Ecology* 47: 393–407

105. Smith, W.P., Hamel, P.B., & R.P. Ford (1996) Mississippi Alluvial Valley forest conversion: implications for eastern North American avifauna. In: *Proceedings 1993 Annual Conference Southeastern Association of Fish and Wildlife Agencies* 47: 460–469.

106. Twedt, D.J., & C.R. Loesch (1999) Forest area and distribution in the Mississippi Alluvial Valley: implications for breeding bird conservation. *Journal of Biogeography* 26: 1215–1224.

107. Brown, S., Hickey, C., Harrington, B., & R. Gill (2001) United States shorebird conservation plan, 2nd edn. Manomet Center for Conservation Sciences, Manomet

108. Bird Life International (2011) Bird Life's Online World Bird Database: the site for bird conservation. Cambridge: Bird Life International.

109. Ganpule, P., Varu, M., Kapil, V., Zala, K.V., & A. Trivedi (2011) Status and distribution of Great Knot in the Gulf of Kachchh, Gujarat, India *Wader Study Group Bulletin* 118 (3):191-193.

110. Balachandran, S. (1997) Population, status, moult, and measurements of Great Knot wintering in South India. *Stilt* 30: 3–6.

111. Robson, C. (1997) India. *Oriental Bird Club Bulletin* 26: 60–61

112. Twedt, D.J. (2013) Foraging Habitat for shorebirds in South Eastern Missouri and its predicted future availability. *UGSS Staff Research Paper published* 728.

113. Webb, E.B., Smith, L.M., Vrtiska, M.P., & T.G. Lagrange (2010) Effects of local and landscape variables on wetland bird habitat use during migration through the Rainwater Basin. *Journal Wildlife Management* 74: 109–119.

114. Powell, G.N. (1987) Habitat use by wading birds in a subtropical estuary: implications of hydrography. *Auk* 104: 740–749.

115. Taft, O.W., Colwell, M.A., Isola, C.R., & Safran, R.J. (2002) Waterbird responses to experimental drawdown: implications for the multispecies management of wetland mosaics. *Journal of Applied Ecology.* 39: 987–1001.

116. Bolduc, F., & A.D. Afton (2004) Relationships between wintering waterbirds and invertebrates, sediments and hydrology of coastal marsh ponds. *Waterbirds* 27: 333–341.

117. Kingsford, R.T., Jenkins, K.M., & J.L. Porter (2004) Imposed hydrological stability on lakes in arid Australia and effects on waterbirds. *Ecology* 85: 2478–2492.

118. Robertson, D., & T. Massenbauer (2005) Applyisng hydrological thresholds to wetland management for waterbirds, using bathymetric surveys and GIS. In: Zerger, A., Argent, R.M. (Eds.), MODSIM International Congress on Modelling and Simulation. *Modelling and Simulation Society of Australia and New Zealand* Australia, Pp.2407–2413.

119. Holm, T.E., & P. Clausen (2006) Effects of water level management on autumn staging waterbird and macrophyte diversity in three Danish coastal lagoons. *Biodiversity and Conservation* 15: 4399–4423.

120. Straughan, D. (1982) Inventory of the natural resources of sandy beaches in southern California. *Technical Report, Alan Hancock Foundation* 6.

121. Straughan, D. (1983) Ecological characteristics of sandy beaches in the Southern California Bight. Pp.441-447 *in* McLachlan, A. and T. Erasmus (eds.) Sandy Beaches as Ecosystems. Dr. W. Junk, The Hague, The Netherlands.

122. Dugan, J. E., Hubbard, D. M., & H.M. Page (1995) Scaling population density to body size: tests in two soft sediment intertidal communities. *Journal of Coastal Research* 11 (3): 849-857.

123. Dugan, J. E., & D.M. Hubbard (1996) Local variation in populations of the sand crab, *Emerita analoga* (Stimpson) on sandy beaches in southern California. *Revista Chilena de Historia Natural* 69: 579-588.

124. Brown, S., Hickey, C., Gill, B., Gorman, L., Gratto-Trevor, C., Haig, S., Harrington, B., Hunter, C., Morrison, G., Page, G., Sanzen bacher, P., Skagen, S., Warnock, N., National Shorebird Conservation Assessment (2000a): Shorebird Conservation Status, Conservation Units, Population Estimates, Population Targets, and Species Prioritization. Manomet Center for Conservation Sciences, Manomet, MA.

125. Moreira, F. (1993) Patterns of use of intertidal estuarine areas by feeding bird assemblages: a study in the Tagus Estuary. *Ardeola* 40: 39-53.

126. Musgrove, A.J., Langston, R.H.W., Baker, H. & R.M. Ward (eds.) (2003) Estuarine Waterbirds at Low Tide: the WeBS Low Tide Counts 1992/93 to 1998/99. WSG, *BTO, RSPB, JNCC*, Thetford.

127. Murkin, H.R., & J.A. Kadlec (1986) Relationships between waterfowl and macroinvertebrates densities in a northern prairie marsh. *Journal of Wildlife Manage* 50: 212-217.

128. Colwell, M.A., & S.L. Landrum (1993) Nonrandom shorebird distribution and fine-scale variation in prey abundance. *Condor* 95: 94-103.

129. Safran, R.J., Isola, C.R., Colwell, M.A., & O.E. Williams (1997) Benthic invertebrates at feeding locations of nine waterbird species in managed wetlands of the northern San Joaquin Valley, California. *Wetlands* 17: 407-415.

130. Cardona, L., Royo, P., & X. Torras (2001) Effects of leaping grey mullet *Liza saliens* (Osteichthyes, Mugilidae) in the macrophyte beds of oligohaline Mediterranean coastal lagoons. *Hydrobiologica* 462: 233–240.

131. Placyk, J.S., & B. A. Harrington (2004) Prey abundance and habitat use by migratory shorebirds at coastal stopover sites in Connecticut. *Journal field Ornithology* 75 (3): 223–231.

132. Burton, N.H.K., Rehfisch, M.M. & N.A. Clark (2002) Impacts of disturbance from construction work on the densities and feeding behaviour of waterbirds using the intertidal mudflats of Cardiff Bay, UK. *Environmental Management* 30: 865-871.

133. Lafferty, K.D. (2001a) Disturbance to wintering western snowy plovers. *Biological Conservation* 101: 315–325.

134. Connors, P.G., Myers, J.P., Connors, C.S.W., & F.A. Pitelka (1981) Interhabitat movements by Sanderlings in relation to foraging profitability and the tidal cycle. *The Auk* 98: 49-64.

135. Drake, K.R., Thompson, J.E., Drake, K.L., & C. Zonick (2001) Movements, habitat use and survival of nonbreeding Piping Plovers. *The Condor* 103: 259-267.

136. Ribeiro, P.D., Iribarne, O.O., Navarro, D., & L. Juareguy (2004) Environmental heterogeneity, spatial segregation of prey, and the utilization of southwest Atlantic mudflats by migratory shorebirds. *Ibis* 146: 672-682.

137. Warnock, S.E., & J.Y. Takekawa (1995) Habitat preferences of wintering shorebirds in a temporally changing environment-western sandpipers in the SFB estuary. *Auk* 112: 920-930.

138. Spencer J (2001) Migratory shorebird ecology in the Hunter estuary, South Eastern Australia PhD thesis, Australian Catholic University 143 pp

139. Aarif, KM Muzaffar, S.B Babu S and Prasadan P.K (2014) Shorebird assemblages respond to anthropogenic stress by altering habitat use in a wetland in India. *Biodiversity and Conservation* 23 (3) 727-740

140. Aarif, K.M. Prasadan, P.K. Basheer P.M. and Abdul Hameed S.V. (2015). Population trends of wintering gulls in the Kadalundi-Vallikkunnu Community Reserev, Southern India *Journal of Environmental Biology:* 36(4)597-600

141. Aarif K.M and Prasadan P.K (2014) Injured migratory shorebirds and gulls in the Kadalundi-Vallikkunnu Community Reserve. *Journal of Environmental Biology* 35: (1) 243-246.

142 Aarif K.M and Prasadan P.K (2014) Conservation issues of KVCR, the wintering ground and stop–over site of migrant shorebirds in south west coast of India *Biosystamatica* 8 (1/2) 51-57.

143. Musale, A.S., & D. Desai (2010) Distribution and abundance of macrobenthic polychaetes along the South Indian Coast. *Environment Monitoring Assessment* 3: 1701-1713.

144. Parulekar, A. H., & A. B. Wagh (1975) Quantitative studies on benthic macrofauna of north-eastern Arabian Sea shelf. *Indian Journal of Marine Sciences* 4: 174– 176.

145. Harkantra, S. N., Nair, A., Ansari, Z. A., & A.H. Parulekar (1980) Benthos of the shelf region along the west coast of India. *Indian Journal of Marine Sciences* 9:106–110.

146. Ingole, B. S., Rodrigues, N., & Z. A. Ansari (2002) Macrobenthic communities of the coastal waters of Dabhol, west coast of India. *Indian Journal of Marine Sciences* 31 (2): 93–99.

147. Sekar, V., Rajasekaran, R., Prithiviraj, N., Muthukumaravel, K., & Oliva (2012) Correlative study on Polychaetes assessment assistance of Environmental parameter in littoral areas of velar estuary, South East Coast of India. *Journal Fernando* 4 (11): 337-342.

148. Aarif KM (2015) Ecology and foraging behaviour of some migrant shorebirds in the Kadalundi-Vallikkunnnu Community Reserve on the west coast of India. PhD thesis, Kannur University 221 pp

149. Rajpar, M.N., & M. Zakaria (2011) Effects of water level fluctuation on waterbirds distribution and aquatic vegetation composition at natural

wetland resources, Peninsular Malaysia. *International Scholarly Research Network* 1-13.

150. Siriwardena, G.M., Baillie, S.R., Buckland, S.T., Fewster, R.M., Marchant, J.H., & J.D. Wilson (1998) Trends in the abundance of farmland birds: a quantitative comparison of smoothed common birds census indices. *Journal of Applied Ecology* 35 (1): 24–43.

151. Ingole, B. S., Rodrigues, N., & Ansari, Z. A. (2002). Macrobenthic communities of the coastal waters of Dabhol, west coast of India. *Indian Journal of Marine Sciences, 31*(2), 93–99.

152. Kaminski, M.R., Baldassarre, G. A., & A.T. Pearse (2006) Waterbird responses to hydrological management of wetlands reserve program habitats in New York, *Wildlife Society Bulletin* 34 (4): 921–926.

153. Basu, A., Sengupta, S., Dutta, S., Saha, A., Ghosh, P., & S. Roy (2013) Studies on macrobenthic organisms in relation to water parameters at East Calcutta Wetlands. *Journal of Environmental Biology* 34: 733-737.

154. Idowu, E.O., & A.A.A. Ugwumba (2005) Physical, Chemical and benthic faunal characterstics of a southern Nigeria reservoir. *The Zoologist* 3: 15-25.

155 Gray, J. S. (1981) The ecology of marine sediments. An introduction to the structure and function of benthic communities. In: *Cambridge studies in modern biology* (p. 185). Cambridge University Press.

156. Gray, J.S. (1974) Animal–sediment relationships. *Oceanography Marine Biology Annual Review* 12: 223–261

157. Buchanan, J.B. (1984) Sediment analysis. In: Holme, N.A., & A.D. McIntyre (Eds.), Methods for the Study of Marine Benthos. Blackwell Scientific Publications, Oxford and Edinburgh, pp. 41-65.

158. Creutzberg, F., Wapenaar, P., Duineveld, G., & N. Lopez (1984) Distribution and density of benthic fauna in the southern North Sea in relation to bottom characteristics and hydrographic conditions. *Journal du Conseil International pour l'exploration de la* 183: 101-110.

159. Snelgrove, P.V.R., & C.A. Butman (1994) Animal sediment relationships revisited: cause versus effect. *Oceanography and Marine Biology: An Annual Review* 32: 111 - 177.

160. Ansari, Z. A. (1977) Macrobenthos of the Cochin backwater. *Mahasagar-Bulletin of the National Institute of Oceanography* 10 (3 & 4): 169–171.

161. Gray, J.S. (1981) The ecology of marine sediments. An tntroduction to the structure and function of benthic communities. In: Cambridge studies in modern biology 185p. Cambridge University Press.

162. Meksumpun, C., & S. Meksumpun (1999) Polychaete–sediment relations in Rayong, Thailand. *Environmental Pollution* 105: 447–456.

163. Sanders, H.L., Grassle, J.F., Hampson, G.R., Morse, L.S., Garner Price, S., & C.C. Jones (1980) Anatomy of an oil spill: long term effects of the grounding of the barge Florida off West Falmouth, Massachusetts. *Journal of Marine Research* 38: 265–380.

164. Reeder, W.G. (1951) Stomach analysis of a group of shorebirds. *Condor* 53: 43-45.

165. Rundle, W.D. (1982) A case for esophageal analysis in shorebird food studies. *Journal of Field Ornithology* 55: 249-257.

166. Akiyama, A. (1988) Birds in tidal flats, in Ecology and Eco-technology in Estuarine-Coastal Area Ed by Y Kurihara: Tokai University Press, Tokyo, 98–108.

167. Liang, S.H., Shieh, B.S., & Y.S. Fu (2002) A structural equation model for physiochemical variables of water, benthic invertebrates, and feeding activity of waterbirds in Sitsao Wetlands of southern Taiwan. *Zoological Studies* 41: 441–451.

168. Courtney, L.A., & W.H. Clements (1998) Effects of acidic pH on benthic macroinvertebrates communities in microcosms. *Hydrobiologia* 379: 135-145.

169. Leland, H.V., & S.V. Fend (1998) Benthic invertebrate distribution in the San Joaquin River, California, in relation to physical and chemical factors. *Canadian Journal of Fish and Aquatic Science* 55: 1051-1067.

170. McRae, G., Camp, D.K., Lyons W.G., & T.L. Dix (1998) Relating benthic infaunal community structure to environmental variables in estuaries using non-metric multidimensional scaling and similarity analysis. *Environment Monitoring Assessment* 51: 233-246.

171. Halliday, J. B., Curtis, D. J., Thompson, D. B. A., Bingal, E. M., & J. C. Smyth (1982) The abundance and feeding distribution of Clyde Estuary shorebirds. *Scottish Birds* 12: 65–72.

172. Weber, L. M., & S.M. Haig (1997) Shorebird diet and size selection of nereid polychaetes in South Carolina coastal diked wetlands. *Journal of Field Ornithology* 68: 358–366.

173. Ramenofsky, M. (1990) Fat storage and fat metabolism in relation to migration. *In* Bird Migration: *Physiology and Ecophysiology,* Pp. 214–231.

174. Wingfield, P.C., Schwabl, H., & P.W. Mattocks, Jr. (1990) Endocrine mechanisms of migration. *In* Bird Migration: *Physiology and Eco-physiology* (E. Gwinner, Ed.), Pp. 232–256. Springer- Verlag, Berlin.

175. Jenni, L., & S. Jenni-Eiermann (1998) Fuel supply and metabolic constraints in migrating birds. *Journal of Avian Biology* 29: 521–528.

176. Piersma, T. (1998) phenotypic flexibility during migration: Optimization of organ size contingent on the risks and rewards of fueling and flight? Journal of *Avian Biology* 29: 511–520.

177. Myers, J.P., Morrison, R.I.G., Antas, P.Z., Harrington, B.A., Lovejoy, T.E., Sallaberry, M., Senner, S.E., & A. Tarak (1987) Conservation strategy for migratory species. *American Scientist* 75: 19–26.

178. Piersma, T.R., Hoekstra, A., Dekinga, A., Koolhaas, P., Wolf, P., Battely, & P. Wirsma (1993b) Scale and intensity of intertidal habitat use by Knots in the Western Wadden Sea in relation to food, friends and foes. *Netherlands Journal of Sea Research* 31: 331-357.

179. Piersma, T., Reneerkens, J., & M. Ramenofsky (2000) Baseline Corticosterone Peaks in Shorebirds with Maximal Energy Stores for Migration: A General Preparatory Mechanism for Rapid Behavioral and Metabolic Transitions. *General and Comparative endocrinology* 120: 118-126.

180. Mercier, F., & R. McNeil (1994) Seasonal variations in intertidal density of invertebrate prey in a tropical lagoon and effects of shorebird predation. *Canadian Journal of Zoology* 72: 1755–1763.

181. Sanchez, M.I., Green, A.J., & E.M. Castellanos (2006) Spatial and temporal fluctuations in presence and use of chironomid prey by shorebirds in the Odiel saltpans, south-west Spain. *Hydrobiologia* 567: 329–340.

182. Zou, F.S., Zhang, H.H., Dahmer, T., Yang, Q.F., Cai, J.X., Zhang, W., & C. Liang (2008) The effects of benthos and wetland area on shorebird abundance and species richness in coastal mangroves wetlands of Leizhou Peninsular, China. *Forest Ecology and Management* 255: 3813-3818.

183. Kuwae, T., Miyoshi, E., Sassa, S., & Y. Watabe (2010) Foraging mode shift in varying environmental condition by dunlin *Calidris alpine*. *Marine Ecology Progress Series* 406: 281-289.

184. Ens, B.J., Smaal, A.C. & J. de Vlas (2004) The effects of shellfish fishery on the ecosystems of the Dutch Wadden Sea and Oosterschelde; Final report on the second phase of the scientific evaluation of the Dutch shellfish fishery policy (EVA II). Alterra-Report 1011, Wageningen, The Netherlands

185. Leopold, M.F., Dijkman, E.M., Cremer, J.S.M., Meijboom, A. & P.W. Goedhart (2004) De effecten vanmechanische kokkelvisserij op de benthische macrofauna en hun habitat. Eindverslag EVA II. Deelproject C1/3. Alterra rapport 955. Alterra, Wageningen, The Netherlands.

186. Van Gils, J.A., Piersma, T., Dekinga, A., Spaans, B., & C. Kraan (2006b) Shellfish dredging pushes a flexible avian top predator out of a marine protected area. *PLoS Biology* 4: 2399–2404.

187. Van Gils, J.A., Kraan, C., Dekinga, A., Koolhaas, A., Drent, J., de Goeij, P., & T. Piersma (2009) Reversed optimality and predictive ecology: burrowing depth forecasts population change in a bivalve. *Biology Letters* 5: 5–8.

188. Kraan, C., Piersma, T., Dekinga, A., Koolhaas, A., & J. van der Meer (2007) Dredging for edible cockles *Cerastoderma edule* on intertidal flats: short-term consequences of fishermen's patch-choice decisions for target and non-target benthic fauna. *ICES Journal of Marine Science* 64: 1735–1742.

189. Raj, V.M., Padmavathy, S., & S. Sivakumar (2013) Water quality Parameters and it influences in the Ennore estuary and near Coastal Environment with respect to Industrial and Domestic sewage. *International Research Journal of Environment Sciences* 2(7): 20-25.

190. Gipson, R.N. (1982) Recent studies on the biology of intertidal fishes, *Oceanography and Marine Biology Annual Review* 20: 363-414.

191. Balasubramanian, R., & L. Kannan (2005) Physico-chemical characteristics of the coral reef Environs of the Gulf of Mannar Biosphere Reserve, India. *International Journal of Ecology and Environmental Science* 31: 265-271.

192. Ramamurthy, S. (1965) Studies on plankton of the north Kanara coast in relation to pelagic fishery. *Journal of Marine Biological Association of India* 7: 127-149.

193. Dehadrai, P.V., & R.M.S. Bhargava (1972) Distribution of chlorophyll, carotenoids and phytoplankton in relation to certain environmental factors along the central west coast of India. *Marine Biology* 17 (1): 30-37.

194. Sarvanane, S., Nandakumar, K., Durairaj, G., & K.V.K. Nair (2000) Plankton as indicators of coastal water bodies during south-west to north-east monsoon transition. *Current Science* 78 (2): 173-176.

195. Madhupratap, M., Nair, K.N.V., Gopalakrishnan, T.C., Haridas, P., Nair, K.K.C., Venugopal, P., & M. Ganus (2001) Arabian Sea oceanography and fisheries of the west coast of India, *Current Science* 81(4): 1-10.

196. Britton, R.H., & A.R. Johnson (1987) An ecological account of a Mediterranean salina: The Salin de Giraud, Camargue (S. France). *Biological Conservation* 42: 185-230.

197. Ramanathan, A.L., Subramanian, V., Ramesh, R., Chidambaram, S., & A. James (1999) Environmental Geochemistry of the pichavaram mangrove ecosystem South East Coast of India. *Environmental Geology* 37 (3): 223-233.

198. Saviour, N.M. (2012) Environmental impact of soil and sand mining a review. *International Journal of Science Environment and Technology* 1 (3): 125-134.

199. Santhosh, S., Sobha, V., & V. Kumar (2008) Textural and geochemical assessment of paravurkappil back water with special reference to sea sand deposition, Southern Kerala. *The Ecoscan,* 2: 187-194.

200. Sandilyan, S., Thiyagesan, K., & R. Nagarajan (2008) Ecotourism in wetlands causes loss of biodiversity. *Current Science* 95: 1511.

201. Burton, N.H.K., Evans, P.R., & M.A. Robinson (1996) Effect on shorebird numbers of disturbance, the loss of a roost site and its replacement by an artificial island at Hartlepool, Cleveland. *Biological Conservation* 77: 193–201.

202. Marsden, S.J. (2000) Impact of disturbance on waterfowl wintering in a UK dockland redevelopment area. *Environment Mangement* 26: 207–213.

203. Prasanthan, V. (1999) Environmental Impact Assessment: Carbon, Nitrogen, Phosphorus and Major elements of Parvathy Puthen Ar- A preliminary study. *M. Phil thesis*, University of Kerala.

204. Ekong, F., Jacob, A., & P. Uyanga (2011) Pollution Levels of Coastal Water Resources and the Socio-economic Effects on Iko Communities in Akwa Ibom State. *Journal of Human Ecology* 1: 41-46.

205. Pienkowski, M.W. (1983b) The effects of environmental conditions on feeding rates and prey-selection of shore plovers. *Ornis Scandinavian* 14: 227–238.

206. Schell & Krekes (1989) Distribution abundance and biomass of benthic macroinvertebrates in relation to pH and nutrients in eight lakes, Nova Scotia, Canada. *Water Air Soil Pollution* 46: 354-474.

207. Sonal, D., Jagruti, R., & P. Geeta (2010) Avifaunal diversity and water quality analysis of an inland wetland. *Journal of Wetlands Ecology* 4: 1-32.

208. Moyle, J.B. (1949) Some indices of lake productivity. *Trans American Fish Society* 76: 332-334.

209. Geetha, P.N., Thasneem, T.A., & S.B. Nandan (2010) Macrobenthos and its relation to ecosystem dynamics in the Cochin estuary. *Lake 2010:* Wetlands, *Biodiversity and Climate Change conference* 1-12 pp

210. Islam, S.M., Sikar Azim, N.M., Imran, A.M., Hussain, B.M., Malick, D., & M.M. Morshed (2013) Intertidal macrobenthic fauna of the Karnafuli estuary; relation with environmental variables. *World Applied Science Journal* 21 (9): 1366-1377

211. Hutchinson, G.E. (1957) A Treatise on Limnology. L Geography, Physics and Chemistry. John Wiley and Sons, New York, 1015p.

212. Wetzel, R.G. (1975) Limnology. *Saunders* Philadelphia, 743p.

213. Nilsson, S.G., & I.N. Nilsson (1978) Breeding bird community densities and species richness in lakes. *Oikos* 31: 219-221

214. Richardson, C.J., Tiltol, D.L., Kadhlee, J.A., Chamie, J.P.M.,& W.A. Wentz (1978) Nutrient dynamics of northern wetland ecosystems in Good. R.E., Whiham D.F. & Simpson.R.L. (eds) Freshwater wetlands: *Ecological process and management potential* 217-292. Newyork: Academic Press.

215. Kuwae, T., Hosokawa, Y., & N. Eguchi (1998) Dissolved inorganic nitrogen cycling in Banzu intertidal sand-flat, Japan. *Journal of Mangroves and Salt Marshes* 2: 167–175.

216. Ochi, T., & H. Takeoka (1986) The anoxic water mass in Hiuchi- Nada part 1. Distribution of the anoxic water mass. *Journal of Oceanographical Society of Japan* 42: 1–11.

217. Kemp, W.M., Sampou, P.A., Garber, J., Tuttle, J. & W.R. Boynton (1992) Seasonal depletion of oxygen from bottom waters of Chesapeake Bay: roles of benthic and Planktonic respiration and physical exchange processes. *Marine Ecology Progress Series* 85: 137–152.

218. Rosenberg, R., & L.O. Loo (1988) Marine eutrophication induced oxygen deficiency: effects on soft bottom fauna, western Sweden. *Ophelia* 29: 213–225.

219. McKnight, D.E., & J.B. Low (1969) Factors affecting waterfowl production on a spring-fed salt marsh in Utah. *Trans North American Wildlife Conference* 34: 307-314.

220. Schroeder, L. D. (1973) A literature review on the role of invertebrates in waterfowl management. *Colombo Division of Wildlife Species Report* Pp.13-29.

221. Swanson, G.A., & M.I. Meyer (1973) The role of invertebrates in the feeding ecology of anatidae during the breeding season. (Pp.143-185 in Waterfowl Habitat Management Symposium, Moncton, New Brunswick)

222. Kaminski, R.M., & H.H. Prince (1981) Dabbling duck activity and foraging responses to aquatic macro invertebrates. *The Auk* 98: 115-126.

223. Murkin, H.R., Kaminski, R.M., & R. D. Titman (1982) Responses by dabbling ducks and aquatic invertebrates to an experimentally manipulated cattail marsh. *Canadian Journal of Zoology* 60: 2324–2332.

224. Hafner, H., Dugan, P.J., & V. Boy (1986) Use of artificial and natural wetlands as feeding sites by Little Egrets in the Camargue Southern France. *Colonial Waterbirds* 9: 149-154.

225. Paracuellos, M., 2006, How can habitat selection affect the use of a wetland complex by waterbirds? Biodiversity and Conservation, 15: 4569-4582.

226. Sjoberg, K. (1989) Time related predator or prey interactions between birds and fish in northern Swedish river. *Oecologia* 67: 35-39.

227. Parker, G.R., Petrie, M.J., & D.T. Sears (1992) Waterfowl distribution relative to wetland acidity. *Journal of Wildlife Management* 56: 268-274.

228. Burger, J., & M. Gochfeld (1983) Jamaica Bay studies, Flocking associations of shorebirds at an Atlantic coast estuary. *Biology Behaviour* 8: 289-318.

229. Fitzpatrick, S., & B. Bouchez (1998) Effects of recreational disturbance on the foraging behaviour of wags on ˉa rocky beach. *Bird Study* 45: 157-17.

230. Smit, C.J., & G.J.M. Visser (1993) Effects of disturbance on shorebirds: a summary of existing knowledge from the Dutch Wadden Sea and Delta area. *Wader Study Group Bulletin* 68: 6-19.

231. Thomas, K.K., Vitek, R.G., & C. Bretz (2003) Effects of human activity on the foraging behaviour of sanderlings *Calidris alba. Biological Conservation* 109: 67–71.

232. Evans, P.R. (1989) *Predation of intertidal faunal by waders in relation to time of day, tide and year.* In: Chelazz, G., Vannini, M. (Eds.), North Atlantic Treaty Organization Advanced Research Workshop, 182. Plenum Press, New York.

233. Mitchell, J.R., Moser, M.E., & J.S. Kirby (1989) Declines in midwinter counts of waders roosting on the Dee Estuary. *Birds Study* 35: 191-198.

234. Stein, R.H., & J.J. Magnuson (1976) Behavioural response of the crayfish to a fish predator. *Ecology* 57: 751-761.

235. Yasue, M. (2006) Environmental factors and spatial scale influence shore bird's responses to human disturbance. *Biological Conservation* 128: 47-54.

236. Cooper, J.M., In: Poole, C.A., & F. Gills (1994) *Least Sandpiper,* (115). Academy of Natural Sciences, Philadelphia.

237. Moskoff, W., & Montgomerie, R., InPoole, C.A., & F. Gills (2001) *Baird's Sandpiper* 66: Academy of Natural Sciences, Philadelphia

238. Zwarts, L. (1972) Verstoring van wadvogels. *Waddenbull* 7: 7-12.

239. Kooy, A., Koersveld, S., & M. Suy (1975) De invloed van recreatie en andere verstoringsbronneno p de avifauna van het eiland Vlieland. Unpubl. report Vakgroep Natuurbeheer L.H. Wageningen, Nr. 335.

240. Anderson, G.M. (2003) Investigations into shorebird community ecology: interrelations between morphology, behaviour, habitat and abiotic factors. MSc dissertation, University of Auckland 215p.

241 Kober, K. (2004) Foraging ecology and habitat use of wading birds and shorebirds in the mangrove ecosystems of the Caete Bay, Breman Brazil *PhD thesis* 192p.

242 Finn, G. P. (2009) Habitat selection, foraging ecology and conservation of Eastern Curlews on their non- breeding grounds. *PhD thesis*, Griffith University 179 pp.

243. Everaert, J., & D. Bauwens (2007) A possible effect of electromagnetic radiation from mobile phone base stations on the number of breeding House Sparrows. *Electromagnetic Biology and Medicine* 26: 63-72.

244. Beason, R.C., & P. Semm (2002) Responses of neurons to an amplitude modulated microwave stimulus. *Neuroscience Letters* 333: 175-178.

245. Balmori, A. (2003) The effects of microwave radiation on the wildlife. Preliminary results, Valladolid, Spain, February. Manuscript submitted for publication to Electromagnetic Biology and Medicine.

246. Balmori, A. (2004) Effects of the electromagnetic fields of phone masts on a population of White Stork, Spain, March. Manuscript submitted for publication to Electromagnetic Biology and Medicine, with figures, diagrams and datasets not in published version 13p.

247. Balmori, A. (2005) Possible effects of electromagnetic fields from phone masts on a population of White Stork. *Electromagnetic Biology and Medicine* 24: 109-119.

248. Manville, A.M., II. (2005) Bird strikes and electrocutions at power lines, communication towers, and wind turbines: state of the art and

state of the science–next steps toward mitigation. Bird Conservation Implementation in the Americas: Proceedings 3rd International Partners in Flight Conference 2002, C.J. Ralph and T.D. Rich (eds.). U.S.D.A. Forest Service General Technical Report PSW-GTR-191, Pacific Southwest Research Station, Albany, CA: 1051-1064.

249. Balmori, A., & O. Hallberg (2007) The urban decline of the House Sparrow: a possible link with electromagnetic radiation. *Electromagnetic Biology and Medicine* 26: 141-151.

250. Lee, H. Y., & S. S. Shih (2004) Impacts of vegetation changes on the hydraulic and sediment transport characteristics in Guandu mangrove wetland. *Ecological Engineering* 23: 85–94.

251. Shao, K.T., Lee, S.C., Maa, C.J., Chen, C.P., Jan, R.Q., Severinghaus, L.L., Jeng, M.S., Hsieh, H.L., Wu, J.T., & C.Y. Chiu (2001) The development of an ecological monitoring system for the Danshuei estuary, the second year report of Academia Sinica Thematic Research Project. *Academia Sinica* Taipei, Taiwan.

252. Parsons, T.R., Takahashi, M., & B. Hargrave (1984) Biological Oceanographic Process. Pergamon Press, London, 332p.

253. Merilainen, M.S. (1998) Meiobenthos in relation to macrobenthic communities in a low saline, partly acidified estuary, Bothnian Bay, Finland. *Annales Zoologici Fennici* 25: 277-292.

254. Sanders, H.L. (1958) Benthic studies in Buzzards Bay. I. Animal sediment relationships. *Limnology Oceanography* 3: 245–258.

255. Pearson, T.H., & R. Rosenberg (1978) Macrobenthic succession in relation to organic enrichment and pollution of the marine environment. *Oceanography Marine Biology Annual Review* 16: 229–311.

256. Lopez, G.R., & J.S. Levinton (1987) Ecology of deposit-feeding animals in marine sediments. *Review Biology* 62: 235–260.

257. Lopez, G., Taghon, G., & J. Levinton (1989) Ecology of marine deposit feeders. Lecture Notes on Coastal and Estuarine Studies 31. Springer New York.

258. Sarda, R., Foreman, K., & I. Valiela (1995) Macroinfauna of a Southern New England salt marsh: seasonal dynamics and production. *Marine Biology* 121: 431-445.

259. Otani, S., Kozuki, Y., Yamanaka, R., Sasaoka, H., Ishiyama, T., Okitsu, Y., Sakai, H., & Y. Yoji Fujiki (2010) The role of crabs (*Macrophthalmus japonicus*) burrows on organic carbon cycle in estuarine tidal flat, Japan. *Estuarine, Coastal and Shelf Science* 86: 434-440

260. Macfarlane, G.R., & D.J. Booth (2001) Estuarine macrobenthic community structure in the Hawkesbury River, Australia relationship with sediment physicochemical and anthropogenic parameters. Journal of *Environmental Monitoring and Assessment* 72: 51–78.

261. Thompson, J.J. (1993) Shorebirds as indicators of habitat type and biodegradation. Pp. 79-82 in C.P Caterall, P. Driscoll, K Hulsman and A Taplin, editors. Birds and their habitats: status and conservation in Queensland. *Queensland ornithological society.*

262. Raffaelli, D., Balls, P., Way, S., Patterson, I.J., Hohmann, S., & N. Corp (1999) Major long-term changes in the ecology of the Ythan estuary, Aberdeenshire, Scotland; how important are physical factors? *Aquatic Conservation* 9: 219–236.

263. Kennish, M. J. (2002) Environmental threats and environmental future of estuaries. *Environmental Conservation* 29: 78–107.

264. Shyamjith and Ramani (2014) Is sand bar formation a major threat to mangrove ecosystems, *International Journal of Science and Research* (3)11: 2005 – 2011.